REFLECTIONS ON ANGER

REFLECTIONS ON ANGER

Women and Men in a Changing Society

CHRISTA REISER

Westport, Connecticut
London

Library of Congress Cataloging-in-Publication Data

Reiser, Christa, 1947–
    Reflections on anger : women and men in a changing society / by
Christa Reiser.
        p.   cm.
    Includes bibliographical references and index.
    ISBN 0–275–95777–2 (alk. paper)
    1. Anger. 2. Anger—Case studies. 3. Man-woman relationships.
4. Man-woman relationships—Case studies. I. Title.
BF575.A5R45   1999
152.4′7—dc21   98–33626

British Library Cataloguing in Publication Data is available.

Library of Congress Catalog Card Number: 98–33626
ISBN: 0–275–95777–2

First published in 1999

Praeger Publishers, 88 Post Road West, Westport, CT 06881
An imprint of Greenwood Publishing Group, Inc.

Printed in the United States of America

The paper used in this book complies with the
Permanent Paper Standard issued by the National
Information Standards Organization (Z39.48–1984).

10 9 8 7 6 5 4 3 2 1

Contents

Preface

When I told people that I was writing a book on men, women, and anger, almost without exception the response was, "That sounds interesting!" The next most common reply—typically from a woman—was along the lines of, "You got a few hours? I could tell you some things!" I suppose this topic seems so interesting because it deals with an area of our lives that we rarely talk about openly. Anger, in both ourselves and others, is at once familiar and alien. Although part of ourselves and our lives, it is rarely closely examined because it makes us uncomfortable, and most of us do our best to get it behind us. This is an emotion that catches us off-guard. The power punch of anger and its potential or actual loss of control make it hard to tarry in its wake.

We may fear anger because we don't understand it. The unrestrained anger hurled at us by a loved person in our life may gouge out small and large chunks of security and trust until we are no longer whole, but we are not sure what to do in response. Although a family may be ravaged by this angry person—as many of those I interviewed testified—this anger does not tend to become a topic for discussion. This silence makes it impossible to understand anger and easy to fear it. Such a situation gives anger more power than it deserves. At its best, anger should simply be a warning, a signal of something gone wrong. We ought to be able to rally as a family or as an individual and ask the angry person, "What is it that is hurting you, threatening you, troubling you?" What can we do to identify and cast out the demons—the fears, disappointments, injustices, worries—that are behind the shouted words, the raised hand, the sarcastic tone, the hurled plate?

By and large the individuals I talked with had no real sense of the origins of anger in their parents. A person would simply state, "My father was an angry man." It was a given, the way it was, regardless of how much damage and hurt derived from the expression of that anger. No one approached and asked the angry person to explain his or her actions. It is easy to understand why people do not do this. We are extremely uneasy with someone who uses anger as a weapon. Also, we are not typically close to such a person; mostly we are tense and afraid. However, our lack of action also reflects our misunderstanding of what anger means. We don't think of it as a warning signal (except for us to take cover) but as an expression of personality. This makes it seem like an unchangeable situation. We don't see the angry person so much as a person in trouble as someone who is powerful and scary. Another unhelpful notion is the belief that when someone is angry, we must have done something to deserve it. This interpretation makes it much more likely that we will be searching and defending our own souls rather than trying to figure out what has gone wrong with the angry person or the situation he or she is in.

It is my sincere hope that this book helps to debunk some of these harmful beliefs. Anger fascinates because it is dangerous, unstable, and misunderstood. Reading about anger and talking to the women and men who allowed me to interview them, as well as others, have increased my understanding of this difficult emotion. I hope this book will do so for you.

Acknowledgments

My heartfelt gratitude extends to the following:

My partner in life and love, Kenneth Ray Wilson, who more than anyone else witnessed the excitement as well as the struggle and frustration over the birth of this book and did so with unfailing patience, support, and encouragement. In our journey together we continue to grow in our capacity to deal constructively with conflict and anger.

My beloved son, Devin, for understanding my need for time and space to work on this book; who tolerated varying states of tension and lack of attention with considerable maturity and good humor; and whose teenage ways provided me with more than one opportunity to practice anger control. It is my fervent hope that he will use anger as a source of insight and empathy rather than a weapon of destruction and pain.

All the members of my family, especially my parents, Hildegard and Sheldon Reiser, my parents-in-law, Susan and Eugene Wilson, and my brother Joe and my sister-in-law Janice, whose faith in me and support of my endeavors is much appreciated.

Snow, Jake, Teaser, Zowie, Fuzzball, and Sassy—my four-legged friends who provided much needed tension relief with their wagging tails, joyous purring, and silly antics.

Various friends, particularly Paula Harrell, Pat Leanhardt, Joyce Stocks, and Olivia Musgrave, who willingly and cheerfully identified people for me to interview and whose interest in the project and supportive comments meant a great deal to me.

All of the women and men who sacrificed some of their precious time to share their thoughts and feelings for absolutely no compensation and those who kept asking me, "When is the book going to come out?"

My chair, Richard Caston, who instituted a research release award that made it possible for me to devote an entire semester to this book with absolutely no other professional obligations. This time was essential to the completion of this book.

Shelia Ellis, Betty Lou White, and Ashley Gibson whose technical support was critical in getting the book done and whose encouragement was truly appreciated.

The many colleagues and friends whose interest and encouragement were helpful in keeping me on track.

My editor, Lynn Taylor, who believed in this project and consistently provided guidance and support and a little leeway when needed.

All the members of the production staff, especially Elizabeth Meagher, who guided the book through its final stages in a most helpful manner.

Part I

Anger: Contextual Issues

Chapter 1

Between Havoc and Hope

We live in a time when tensions between many groups of people crackle across the screens of our everyday lives. We have grown accustomed to this static, and usually manage to ignore the clashes between Serb and Croat, Muslim and Hindu, skinhead and immigrant, black and white.

Another, quieter struggle is going on as well, however. And although it is typically not fought with guns or lawsuits, the tensions run deep, the stakes are high, and there is no place to hide. Women and men across the country, and indeed around the world, are confronting each other as they redefine the divisions of labor and love.

Our culture has depicted men and women as adversaries for many years, as expressed in the old phrase "the battle of the sexes." Although this "war" has been raging for centuries, it has taken on new meanings in our time. Relationships between women and men are undergoing a major redefinition as the ground rules for this old battle change and as our culture shifts toward greater intimacy and equality (Stover and Hope 1993). As tradition collides with present-day views, the resulting conflict manifests itself in gender-based tension, anger, hostility, and sometimes aggression.

Although problems between the sexes have always been part of the human condition, the form, severity, and sources of these problems change constantly. The situation between men and women today is different from that of the past because for the first time, at least in Western history, women have come close to achieving equality with men. For the first time, substantial numbers of women and men support the ideal of equality between the sexes. For the first time, the majority of adult women are working outside the home and earning their own income, although most of them not at levels equal to men. For the first time, women have outvoted men at the polls. For the first time, an international women's conference (held in Beijing in 1995) has openly challenged men's right to use their physical power against women. Over time, many groups of women have cried out for justice and equality, but never before have so many women been in a position of actual and potential power, and never before have feminist goals been shared so widely.

Such new social conditions and challenges to our patriarchal legacy have created havoc even while they have generated hope. The evidence is everywhere: newspapers, books, magazines, television programs, movies, music, talk shows, informal conversations, crime statistics, divorce statistics, rates of delayed marriage, cartoons, greeting cards, political debates, and classroom discussions. All of these commonly reflect some kind of trouble in male-female relationships. Popular television shows such as *Roseanne, Murphy Brown*, and *Home Improvement* explore the minefield of gender issues, primarily through sarcasm; rap songs by groups such as 2 Live Crew depict men's relations with women as violent, exploitative, and hostile; movies such as *Basic Instinct* and *War of the Roses* show that aggression and hostility are not limited to one gender.

In her book *Backlash*, Susan Faludi (1991) observes that in movies from the 1940s to the 1970s, men and women were portrayed as struggling with each other, but their intentions were good. The goal was to understand each other in the hope of bridging the gap between the sexes. An analysis of movies from the late 1980s, however, shows that men and women are no longer trying to figure things out. Often women are either omitted from these films altogether or are relegated to mute, incidental characters. Occasionally, too, a film such as *Thelma and Louise* portrays women as rebelling against the emotional and sexual demands imposed by men.

The Anita Hill–Clarence Thomas sexual harassment hearings, the incidents at the Tailhook convention, the "angry white men" challenging changes in the workplace, and the countless reports of battering and murdering of wives, girlfriends, and lovers (and sometimes husbands and boyfriends) drive home the point that tension and hostility are not limited to the world of make-believe. Faludi (1991) cites government statistics showing that sex-related murders increased 160 percent between 1976 and 1984. At least one-third of the women were killed by their husbands or boyfriends; the majority of that group were murdered shortly after declaring their independence by filing for divorce or leaving home.

Various polls reveal a widespread negative perception of the state of relations between the sexes. A recent nationwide random sample of 3,000 women found that women's attitudes toward men are becoming more critical. In 1970, for example, two-thirds of the women surveyed agreed that "most men are basically kind, gentle, and thoughtful." In 1990, only half of the women surveyed agreed with this statement (Langer 1990). In 1970, 32 percent of the women believed that "most men are basically selfish and self-centered"; in 1990, 42 percent thought so. A poll by *Self* magazine ("He Vs She" 1992) found that 45 percent of single women and 35 percent of married women believed that relations between men and women are generally worse than they were ten years before. The 1993 Southern Focus Poll (Wiggins 1993) asked both southern and nonsouthern adults about relations between men and women, and found that about half of each sample thought the situation between the sexes had grown worse in recent years. In a 1993 study of residents of eastern North Carolina, I found that 50 percent of the women and 43 percent of the men judged relations between women and men as worse today than ten years ago.

This tense state of affairs has been widely publicized. The topic has been headlined in recent issues of *Time, Gentleman's Quarterly,* and the *Utne Reader* with the assumption that things are getting worse, not better. An article in the *Utne Reader* asks, "Have you noticed that American men and women seem angrier at one another than ever? Belligerent superpowers have buried the hatchet, but the war between the sexes continues unabated" (Kipnis and Hingston 1993, 69). The authors point out that events such as the Anita Hill–Clarence Thomas controversy could have been used to promote productive dialogue between the sexes, but instead have "fueled male-female resentment." Instead of reconciliation, the result has been increasing polarization.

Many popular books deal with angry and hostile relations between women and men. *The Men We Never Knew, No Good Men, Men Who Hate Women and the Women Who Love Them, Opening Our Hearts to Men,* and *Successful Women, Angry Men* provide interesting and often valuable insights about the way women and men relate to each other, but most of these are not based on research.

Although the tension between women and men, often due to changing roles, is addressed commonly in popular sources, the research is sparse. Many academic books have been written on gender roles and on the problems of being a female or a male in today's changing world. We have carefully documented changes in women's (more so than men's) attitudes and behaviors over time; volumes have been written about differences and similarities between the sexes; many theories have been offered on the origin and perpetuation of gender inequality; various types of discrimination on several levels of analysis have been identified; our consciousness about sexual aggression has been raised; and we have pondered what the future will bring for the sexes. Few scholars, however, give systematic attention to the role of emotion, specifically anger, in male-female relationships.

Much writing, both popular and academic, focuses on the presumed consequences of anger or hostility, such as rape, murder, spouse abuse, and sexual harassment. Yet in contrast to the vast amount of material on aggressive behaviors, relatively little has been written on anger itself. Averill (1982) states in his book on anger that surveys dealing with ordinary, day-to-day anger can be counted on one hand. Although more research on anger has been done since he wrote this, there is much we don't know. Several recent books deal with anger and gender, but these focus on one sex or the other. Sandra Thomas's (1993) book, for example, is called *Women & Anger*. An earlier book by Anthony Astrachan (1986) is titled *How Men Feel*. Yvette Walczak (1988) has written *He and She, Men in the Eighties*. Some authors have explored strong negative feelings of hostility and hatred in works such as *My Enemy, My Love* by Judith Levine (1993) and *Misogynies* by Joan Smith (1992). Both of these books are from a woman's perspective.

Anger is an important emotion with enormous interpersonal consequences, both positive and negative. Sandra Thomas (1993) states that love and anger are the two most powerful emotions in America today. Increasingly, however, it seems that we are speaking the language of anger and aggression rather than the language of love. Anger must be studied in the context of gender relations so we can learn how to reduce it, manage it, and move forward to gender peace. We need to learn how much and what kind of anger has been generated by the tensions accompanying change in gender roles for both women and men, which issues are the most troublesome for both, how women and men deal with feelings and expressions of anger, and how their perceptions of each other contribute to the dynamics of anger.

This book explores the expression, extent, sources, and perceptions of anger in women's and men's lives as they cope with changing definitions of masculinity and femininity, maleness and femaleness, and structural changes in our society. The focus is on understanding what happens on an emotional level as women and men embark on new paths toward intimacy and fulfillment. It is important to study both women and men because their lives are increasingly intertwined. Each group's perceptions of themselves and of the other are crucial in advancing the cause of gender peace. In view of the dramatic changes in gender roles, the apparently high levels of tension and anger between women and men today, and the importance of anger in our lives, it is imperative to integrate the study of anger with the study of gender roles.

In-depth interviews with fifty individuals (twenty-five women and twenty-five men) form the basis of this book. As Averill (1982) advises, "Ultimately...questions regarding the nature and significance of anger must be addressed on the level of everyday experience" (157) because that is where anger has the greatest influence. Thus, to understand the dynamics of anger—meanings, expressions, and perceptions—it is imperative to listen to individuals' own descriptions.

The study of people's definitions and interpretations is critical for understanding human behavior (Shott 1979). It is essential to analyze the degree of fit between perception of self and perception of others. Our reality is ultimately defined by what we believe to be true. It could be, for example, that neither sex feels much anger toward the other, but that each thinks the other is angry toward their own sex. The consequences of this belief, even if it is false, are no less serious than if it is true.

This book is divided into two parts. The first part, chapters 1 through 4, provides a background for understanding anger; both in the context of gender relations and in a more general sense. The second part of the book, chapters 5 through 9, presents the content of the interviews and conclusions.

Chapter 2 assesses potential sources of conflict, tension, and anger on several levels of analysis. I conclude that social structure as well as interpersonal factors not only permit conflict in gender relations but sometimes encourage it. The third chapter provides background on anger; a brief history of the research on anger is followed by a discussion of the importance of anger in interpersonal relationships. In this chapter I also discuss conceptual and definitional issues. The next chapter starts with a review of research on gender and anger and concludes with a summary of my own quantitative research studies on what I then called "gender hostility."   Chapter 5 describes the interview process and the backgrounds of the participants. Along with typical background characteristics, this chapter also provides a look at the anger background of these women and men. They were asked to talk about what they learned about anger while growing up, what typically happened at home when someone was angry, their past and present modes of anger expression, how often they get angry, and their anger targets. The last section of this chapter describes the beliefs the respondents have about the influence of sex on their own anger expression as well as on anger in general. Chapter 6 describes sources of anger from their own point of view (what angers them about men and women they know and men and women in general) and their perceptions of what makes other women and men angry. The fit or lack of fit between these different sets of perceptions is also addressed in this chapter. Chapter 7 describes the extent of anger experienced by the respondents, as well as their perceptions of others' anger levels. Chapter 8 provides a profile of attitudes toward gender-related changes in our society. The respondents were asked to talk about changes they liked and those they disliked. Finally, chapter 9 reviews significant findings and looks toward the future of gender relations.   The participants' own views of "ideal" ways of dealing with anger, general thoughts on anger, and their suggestions for improving female-male relationships are presented, along with a section on implications of this book's findings for future gender relations.

Chapter 2

Social Dynamics and Gender Anger

The author of a book on gender roles asks, "Why isn't man's best friend woman?" It may be puzzling that dogs seem to be better suited than women to be "man's best friend," but this statement is quite understandable from a sociological perspective. In fact, one could argue that it makes more sense for women and men to be strangers, or at least uneasy acquaintances, than friends.

Tension and conflict between women and men seem newsworthy today, but the history of the relations between the sexes has generally been marked by turbulence, ambivalence, resignation, indifference, and often hostility. Although obviously we were meant to be joined physically, our social, intellectual, and emotional relations have more often resembled a battleground than a meeting ground. Today's social and physical circumstances may be even more conducive to high levels of stress, tension, and potential anger than in the past. The stakes are higher than ever before because women and men approach each other with greater equality (and hence more evenly balanced resources and power) and higher expectations. At the same time, the sexes face unprecedented patterns of living that make it impossible to draw on past experience for guidance. To understand the current tension between women and men, we must examine a variety of factors, from broad historical sociocultural forces to interpersonal and psychological factors at the microlevel.

BROAD CULTURAL AND STRUCTURAL CHANGES

For most of recorded history, men and women have not regarded each other as equals or as friends. It was assumed that women and men were dissimilar, even opposites, and that males were superior, a situation that made trust and understanding very difficult. Social historians tell us that for most of human history in most places, men and women have come together for practical, political, and sexual purposes rather than for emotional closeness, respect, and love. The home was primarily a place of work; husbands, wives, and children all participated to make this economic unit efficient. People had little time and incentive to relate to each other in ways that would further the modern goals of emotional intimacy, support, and equality. Edward Shorter's (1975) writings on European family life make it clear that the bonds connecting parents with children and husbands with wives were practical; people needed each other to survive. Wives were considered less valuable than livestock, as illustrated in the expression, "Lucky is the man whose wife is dead and whose horse is alive" (Shorter 1975). The more tender emotions, such as affection and love, were reserved for same-sex friends.

Over a period of 300 years occurred a series of changes that transformed relations between the sexes as large, public, economically based patriarchal family units gave way to small, private, emotionally based, more egalitarian units (Stover and Hope 1993). Once love and affection were incidental to a marriage; today they are almost obligatory. Increasingly, women and men have turned to each other for more intangible satisfactions. Although the norms for the modern family stress equal authority of husband and wife, it was not until the middle of the twentieth century that we began talking seriously about equality—at home, at work, at play. This dialogue (or perhaps dispute), in full swing today, has grown increasingly heated as each party seeks to maintain or gain a more favorable position.

An analogy using a pair of siblings can be applied here. Imagine that for many years, one had more privileges than the other. As long as both siblings accepted this situation, they got along reasonably well, but conflict arose when it occurred to the less privileged sibling that this arrangement was unfair. Although the less privileged sibling might convince the other that his or her cause is just, long-held habits and beliefs are difficult to abandon. Those in the privileged position feel that gains by the less privileged are made at their own expense. This zero-sum view of rights and resources is especially powerful in the United States, where competition is emphasized over cooperation. When siblings fight with each other, some authority figure, such as a parent, usually intervenes. In the war between the sexes, however, there is no equivalent authority figure.

The structured gender inequality and the lack of emotional intimacy that existed for most of human history may seem undesirable from a modern viewpoint, but they kept levels of male-female conflict and marital dissolution low. Institutional incentives and sanctions made it difficult for women to do anything but submit to the authority of their fathers and husbands. They had few reasonable alternatives, or none at all. When conflict arose, simple, clear-cut rules existed to deal with it.

With increasing equality, the potential for both intimacy and conflict has increased. Janet Chafetz summarizes the basic contradiction neatly:

Ironically, the very intimacy that equality fosters probably encourages honesty and openness, which demand expression of disagreement as well as support and agreement. Once conflicts emerge, there is no simple resolution process available. Authority is no longer automatically granted to one spouse, and the power resources of spouses who are equal essentially cancel each other out. (1989, 153)

Popular perceptions parallel Chafetz's thinking. In a Gallup poll of 501 married women, 41 percent "agreed strongly" and 17 percent "agreed" that "increasing equality between men and women will inevitably increase conflict between them" ("He Vs She" 1992). Unmarried women's responses were slightly more pessimistic: 43 percent "agreed strongly" and 20 percent "agreed" with this statement.

Thus, we find ourselves in a somewhat strange social situation today. Just and loving relations between women and men are emphasized more strongly than ever before yet dissatisfaction, resentment, and hostility seem widespread. Our rising expectations have made previously acceptable behavior (such as wife beating) into crimes and have created an atmosphere in which speaking harshly and looking lewdly at members of the other sex are grounds for social and sometimes legal sanction. According to Chafetz (1989), we must accept more overt conflict and acknowledge that such conflict is difficult to resolve if we want full intimacy as a goal. "The same set of social forces that produces what most of us define as a social 'good'—increased intimacy among spouses—also produces heightened levels of marital conflict and divorce" (154). Chafetz also points out that if we accept this analysis, we must recognize that not all problems between men and women can be resolved at the individual level. Thus, in trying to make relations between women and men more equitable and more intimate, we have forfeited some of the stability that characterized more traditional relationships.

These tensions in love and marriage have been exacerbated by other changes. One of the defining characteristics of our time is our society's emphasis on individualism. In the extreme case, people pursue their own pleasures and dreams without a sense of obligation or commitment to others; whatever is needed to achieve personal wealth, pleasure, or power is acceptable. Americans today believe they have a right to choose whatever suits them best. If our own feelings and attitudes are paramount in any given situation, if we have no sense of a greater good, our decisions will be based on individual desire, persuasiveness, or power. Accordingly, if women and men aspire to the same goals and values in a relationship, each will try to have his or her own way, or else they will decide to live apart. Changes in laws, new working patterns, and new norms stressing the value of each individual provide women with the resources and the motivation to leave unhappy relationships. Aaron Kipnis and Elizabeth Herron, the authors of *Gender War, Gender Peace* (1994), believe that much of the "gender war" has been about women and men seeking more choices and wanting their own way. There is too much competition and jealousy between them—too much sibling rivalry, the authors claim.

Economic, technological, and demographic changes have spawned many conditions that provide both opportunities for and obstacles to harmonious male-female relationships. When industrialization caused the separation of work and home, a substantial proportion of women and men spent most of their waking hours apart. Men specialized in earning income away from home, women in taking care of the household and children. Today, women's and men's lives are becoming increasingly intertwined again as more and more women have joined men in the labor force. Both sexes must adjust to this situation. Joan Smith (1992) claims that the presence of women in the workplace transforms it from a neutral into a sexual space: men no longer have a refuge from women. The workplace then becomes a potential setting for sexual games, although the playing field may not be level.

Anthony Astrachan (1986) interviewed men from various backgrounds and found high levels of anger, fear, and envy as a result of changing gender roles—specifically, women's entry into the workplace. Astrachan describes three negative behavior patterns exhibited by his male respondents. The most obvious pattern, he says, is hostility, either "gross and physical or subtle and Machiavellian" (15). A second response is denial of women's competence and power. Third, men felt compelled to transform women into something they can deal with, such as whores. Astrachan believes that men "lose [their] identities, [their] selves, [their] very humanity when women show they can do the same work or exercise the same power." He acknowledges that women also feel pain as they work through the changes, but he thinks that men feel "heavier pain and longer because [they] were usually the beneficiaries of privilege and sometimes of power under the old system" (200).

In a society that forbids employers to discriminate against women and in which it is increasingly difficult for males to provide adequately as breadwinners, women have increased incentives to earn income and strengthen their social position in male-female relationships. Although this historically new situation works toward equalizing resources between men and women, it can also be a significant source of tension and anger until both sides adjust. Too many men (and some women) still view women's advances on economic, political, and intellectual fronts as "annexing men's turf" (Levine 1993, 394).

As a result of the sexual revolution, with its more lenient attitudes and the availability of fairly effective contraceptives, high levels of premarital sex beginning at younger ages have brought the sexes together before they are ready for such a responsibility. They have not yet learned to relate to each other as human beings, much less as sexual beings or potential parents. Misunderstandings and exploitative behaviors and attitudes seem to be common; these fuel resentment, anger, hostility, and sometimes aggression.

High levels of divorce, cohabitation, and postponed marriage have made heterosexual relationships less stable and less formalized than in the past. Many women and men are no longer subject to the legal and moral injunctions that accompany marriage. This situation provides both more freedoms and more vulnerabilities. On the one hand, women have greater opportunities for independence; on the other they lose some of the financial and emotional security associated with marriage. This situation is fraught with ambivalence and frustration.

The highest levels of education in history, coupled with the longest life expectancy, give us the motivation and the time to go beyond parochial views of the world and relationships and examine what has been, what is, and what could be. Education expands us in many ways, but it also breeds dissatisfaction because it shows us alternatives. Through education, we have learned that gender role arrangements are based primarily on culture rather than on biology. This knowledge has removed a major obstacle to change.

PATTERNS OF SOCIALIZATION

The messages that are conveyed to girls and boys also raise barriers between the sexes. Modern, egalitarian expectations for adult male-female relationships are not reflected in socialization practices, which remain fairly traditional. How does one make the transition from an essentially sex-segregated youth where one still learns that it is better to be male, to an adulthood in which the two sexes are supposed to be close emotionally, physically, intellectually, socially, spiritually, and practically? It seems that we either must change the way we bring up boys and girls or give up our goals of love and intimacy based on equality. To preserve the status quo is to invite frustration.

In *Misogynies*, Joan Smith (1992) claims that the "state of covert warfare between the sexes" starts at birth with "the forced march of the sexes into two opposed camps." She believes that we use masculine and feminine behaviors as the way to enforce an unnatural separation between women and men, with the goal of maintaining an unjust power structure. Judith Levine (1993) emphasizes that gender is not only about being different but also about hierarchy; because men are valued and women are devalued, gender enforces inequality and thus oppression. "Women, in rising up against the injustice of male privilege, did not create the state of hostility between the sexes, but they declared the war" (395). Traditional socialization makes it difficult for men and women to learn the skills and attitudes needed for a modern, equalitarian marriage. It creates an additional barrier by instilling different and often contradictory expectations and desires in men and in women. Thus, elements of the male and the female role in today's culture have disturbing implications for harmony between the sexes.

Julia Wood's (1994) book *Gendered Lives* lists the "prime masculine and feminine directives," as outlined by James Doyle (1989). The first directive of masculinity, "Don't be female," urges males to avoid feminine pursuits at all costs. How can one teach young males to shun anything associated with females and yet grow up to love and respect them? One may not intend to devalue females when admonishing a little boy not to "cry like a girl" ("because they're weak" is the implicit message), but that is a likely result. Perhaps it is no wonder that even today, a nationwide poll of teenagers found that a majority of the boys surveyed said that most of the boys they knew considered themselves better than girls. Most of the girls, however, said the girls they knew viewed boys as their equals (Lewin 1994).

A second command of masculinity is, "Be successful." Although this theme does not jeopardize harmonious female-male relationships in the same way as "Don't be female," it impedes creative, equal partnerships by putting pressure on men to win at any cost and to be successful in "manly" ways. It discourages males from considering full-time parenthood as an option. It also encourages women (and men) to see males as "success objects" (Farrell 1991) and thus it dehumanizes them. In this way, anger and resentment can be generated on both sides; men resent being judged by the size of their paycheck, and women are angry at men who devote little or no time to family and household matters.

"Be aggressive" is a third element of the male role. This directive might have no particular implications for male-female relationships if females were off-limits as targets of aggression. Women and children, however, perhaps because of their social inferiority and powerless position, seem to be easy and frequent targets of sexual and physical aggression. Much of the female anger toward males is due to the male attitude that he "can do whatever he wants to her."

Another element of the male role revolves around the injunction, "Be sexual." This expectation, coupled with "Be aggressive," leads to sexual exploitation, with a focus on satisfying men's urges and desires. Wood (1994) observes that this demand makes males as well as females into sex objects because they must "perform" whether or not they want to do so.

The last directive of the male role, according to Doyle, is "Be self-reliant." A "real man" is calm and collected; he doesn't need anything from anyone else. This expectation is translated into frustration and possibly anger in a relationship when the woman wants access to the man's feelings, especially the vulnerable and tender feelings and he is unwilling or unable to share them. It may be good to lean on a rock when one feels weak, but a rock does not invite intimate connections.

These elements of the male role may serve men well in various social and physical situations because they allow them to achieve some goal. When applied to male-female relationships, however, they seem to be destructive rather than beneficial. They encourage men to be self-centered, aggressive, domineering, condescending, and emotionally isolated (Kipnis and Herron 1994). Some of the behaviors associated with masculinity may have invited admiration from women in the past, but today, with the exception of "Be successful," they are more likely to incur women's wrath. Women still expect men to work hard and succeed.

These male directives can be problematic not just in regard to relationships with women, but also in reference to how they fit with social and economic conditions. Helen Hacker (1957) recognized both sources of problems several decades ago when she said:

There are objective indices that all is not well with men. Most obvious is the widespread expression of resentment toward women in conversation, plays, novels, and films. Modern women are portrayed as castrating Delilahs busily leveling men's individuality and invading the strongholds of masculinity in work, play, sex, and the home. (228)

Hacker believed that the "new burdens of masculinity" could stem from several sources. First, it may be more difficult for men to carry out their roles due to the nature of modern conditions; being a successful breadwinner is more difficult due to changes in occupational structure. Problems could also be due to feelings of uncertainty and ambiguity regarding role expectations. Finally, males may find it frustrating to accommodate to the new freedoms and responsibilities of women.

Wood states that the expectations surrounding femininity are more confusing and more conflicting than those associated with the male role, but she identifies five themes. The first theme revolves around physical presentation: "Appearance still counts." Females in our culture are conditioned from infancy to worry about their looks. It is not enough to be neat and clean; one must also be "attractive." In this quest for superficial beauty, the cultivation of inner qualities is often neglected. In relations with men, women either fret that they are not thin enough or pretty enough, or worry that they will lose their looks. Although this expectation causes untold pain, anxiety, and physical harm as females diet and otherwise torture their bodies, it is unclear whether or to what extent this demand contributes to anger between the sexes.

A second element of the female role is, "Be sensitive and caring." This injunction generally results in behaviors and attitudes that nurture and maintain relationships with men (and women) and thus does not generate anger by itself. Problems arise when women refuse to be the emotional caretakers, thus angering men who expect otherwise, or when kind, caring women grow frustrated with men who refuse to reciprocate.

A third theme identified by Wood is "negative treatment of others." Girls learn at an early age that to be female is to be considered inferior by many and that being a girl makes one vulnerable in many ways. In the past, such treatment was most likely to result in low self-esteem, lack of self-confidence, lack of opportunities, depression, and anxiety, but today many females are responding to this expectation with contempt. Although depression rates for females are still high and self-esteem scores too low, increasing numbers of girls are refusing to place themselves or to be placed by others in the category of victim or weakling. These females react with anger to those who might deny them respect and opportunities.

"Be a superwoman" is the fourth commandment of femininity. A woman is expected to do it all: have a career, be a mother, be a wife, keep her youthful shape, smile a lot, and have fun. Such an unrealistic goal can only generate tension, frustration, and perhaps anger, directed either at oneself or at others.

The final principle of femininity is, "There is no longer any single meaning of *feminine*." According to Wood, we are no longer sure exactly what a woman is supposed to be. No matter what a woman chooses to do with her life, she will be applauded by some people and criticized by others. This ambiguity is frustrating, but it also provides new opportunities for self-definition.

Following the dictates of femininity results in women who are sensitive and nurturing but also vain, insecure, and confused, and who try to fulfill everyone's expectations (Kipnis and Herron 1994). Gender role socialization as a whole has several serious implications for relations between women and men. One problem is the lack of fit between the content of gender roles and the new ideals of egalitarian marriages. To a great extent, we are still urging boys and girls to be traditional in outlook and behavior. A second problem is created by the lack of fit between the themes of men's and women's gender roles. When the two sets of expectations are placed side by side, it seems that the resulting behaviors and attitudes are not conducive to loving, trusting, respectful relationships between the sexes. These sets of expectations create a social situation filled with potential strife, disappointment, misunderstanding and frustration.

In an article on male-female conflict among blacks, Clyde Franklin (1989) applies this type of analysis to sources of conflict. He identifies "sex-role noncomplementarity" among black males and females as one major source, arguing that black women are socialized both to be independent (because "you won't find a black man to take care of you") and to make their highest achievement finding a man to take care of her. These contradictory goals lead to an androgynous orientation: black women value aggressiveness and independence, as well as expressiveness and nurturance. Black men also internalize two conflicting messages during childhood. One message stresses the importance of being aggressive, decisive, responsible, and even violent when necessary. The other message warns them that they can't be too aggressive and dominant because they are black and "the man will cut you down" (369). The outcome is men who enact the aggressive, sexist, violent aspects of the male role but are hesitant or passive in regard to the more "productive" aspects, such as being aggressive or decisive in the workplace. Thus the stage is set for conflict when black females and males come together. The women feel exploited and dominated; the men feel that the women don't respect or need them.

Franklin also discusses what he calls "structural" barriers that contribute to male-female conflict among blacks. Black males' limited resources and societal rewards, as well as their high rates of mortality, suicide, incarceration, and unemployment, "render millions of black males socially impotent and/or socially dysfunctional" and "primed for conflictual relationships with black women" (370). A recent article in *Newsweek* reiterates some of Franklin's thoughts. Ellis Cose (1995), the author of the article and the book on which the article is based, recounts many black men's negative experiences and feelings about their place in society and how black women treat them. He cites poll results showing that a substantial portion of black men feel that black women should give up positions of leadership so as not to undermine black men. Many black women resent this view and the more explicitly "macho" or "cool pose" that makes women feel worthless and used. Cose cautions readers, however, about stereotyping all black men as macho and self-absorbed. Many black men are hard-working, responsible husbands and fathers who do not abuse women. He also points out that males of all races have problems with fragile egos and confused thinking, which interfere with fulfilling male-female relationships.

We need to learn to temper or eradicate the excesses of feminine and masculine dictates. Kipnis and Herron (1994) point out that what the sexes love and admire about each other is strikingly similar to what they hate and fear. For example, women admire men's strength and competence but fear their power to control and dominate; men love women's gentleness and appreciate their receptivity but disparage them for being too emotional and overly sensitive. It seems that one way to correct these distortions is to strengthen men's and women's sense of security and power. A woman who feels strong and competent herself is unlikely to fear strength and competence in another. A man who acknowledges his own gentleness and sensitivity is unlikely to belittle it in others.

A passage in Pat Conroy's *The Prince of Tides* (1991) reads as follows: "I have tried to understand women, and this obsession has left me both enraged and ridiculous. The gulf is too vast and oceanic and treacherous. There is a mountain range between the sexes with no exotic race of Sherpas to translate the enigmas of those deadly slopes that separate us" (110). To reduce this gulf, we must revise our patterns of gender role socialization so that we achieve internal and external consistency. These patterns must become symmetrical to reduce emotional and sexual tensions (Lorber 1994). If we want women and men to be friends and lovers in an egalitarian authority structure, we must encourage the behaviors and attitudes that make such relations possible. Judith Lorber (1994) states that the strongest relationships exist between two people who are not only lovers but also friends. If we think women and men have had (and always will have) opposing interests that lead to struggles for dominance and power (Sapiro 1990), we might as well resign ourselves to the war of the sexes.

It would also be helpful if young people today had access to realistic, clear role models. Such models, combined with a clear vision for future male-female relationships, would enable individuals to make choices that allow them to achieve their goals. Many of my students, for example, want an "equal" and loving marriage but are not sure what "equality" entails. Most of them have internalized the modern values of love, equality, and intimacy but have no concrete, realistic ideas for achieving these abstract goals. Most admit that they personally know few couples, or none at all, who have truly good, egalitarian marriages. This situation adds another strand to their anger. Men and women come together with unrealistic and vaguely defined goals; when the honeymoon ends, they are lost. At this stage it is tempting to be angry and place all the blame on the other.

MICROLEVEL DYNAMICS

Some theorists believe that regardless of time or place, hostility or anger toward the opposite sex will exist because it is the result of largely psychological needs or fears over which we have little or no control. The research typically focuses on explaining men's antipathy toward women. It almost seems as though women are not considered capable of harboring strong negative feelings, such as anger or hostility, toward men. Stark-Adamec and Adamec (1982), for example, offer a "fear and loathing hypothesis," which states that hostility toward women is the result of men's fear of menstruation, pregnancy, and female sexuality, as well as their own emotional dependence on women. Betty Friedan (1985, 573) also situates the source of male-to-female hostility in "their very dependence on our love, from those feelings of need that men aren't supposed to have." Smith (1992) believes that men cannot cope with emotions and thus blame women for their own failings, inadequacies, and anger. Others have written about men's traumatic socialization experiences which result from having to distance themselves emotionally and physically from mothers leaving men with feelings of alienation and strong, negative feelings toward women.

Some researchers have attempted to explain women's negative attitudes toward men. Melani and Fodaski (1974) believe that hostility toward men is inevitable because men have more power than women. Levine (1993) depicts relations between the sexes as existing on a battlefront "where a gain for men is a loss for women, and vice versa" (394) a situation that breeds hatred toward both sexes.

Equity theory (Walster, Walster, and Berscheid 1978) holds that inequitable relationships, involving either too little or too much benefit, lead to distress for the participants. Susan Sprecher (1986) found that the negative emotions most closely related to inequity are anger, hurt, and resentment for men and sadness, frustration, and anger for women. Anger was found to be related most closely to both underbenefiting and overbenefiting inequity for the men. Women reported different emotions: they reacted with anger to overbenefiting inequity and with feelings such as depression to underbenefiting inequity.

ANGER AS A RESPONSE

Many of the conditions and changes discussed above can lead to frustration for both women and men. As women feel freer to define life according to their own desires and terms, relations between the sexes have become more openly concerned with power and control. Because of the breakdown in traditional patterns, many women and men no longer know how to handle this situation. Frustrating events can lead to emotional responses other than anger, such as depression, resignation, fear, and anxiety (Baron 1977). Some social analysts (like Andrew Kimbrell) do not view men today as angry and resentful but as sad, powerless, confused, and even self-destructive. They have lost their place as "protectors of family and the earth" and must contend with other men in "the competitive jungle of industrialized society" (Kimbrell 1991, 67). Men today, according to Kimbrell, have no realistic, healthy images of what it means to be a man. Instead they fall prey to the male mystique, which stresses competition, success, and being uncaring and unloving.

As social conditions are changing and basic assumptions are challenged, women and men may be dissatisfied or confused. Certain conditions must be met, however, before anger develops. Carole Tavris (1989) states that we need an interpretive framework or a coherent explanation as well as a vision of alternatives before we can experience anger about frustrating circumstances. She credits the women's movement for forging a connection between private troubles and public issues. As women shifted from blaming themselves or nobody to blaming others, especially men, anger resulted. Today women not only want what they don't have—greater power, more respect, wider choices—but also feel that they deserve these things. Therefore they meet the two conditions that must exist before people feel angry (Tavris 1989).

Given the interconnectedness of women's and men's lives today, it is inevitable that women's inner turmoil and changing expectations will be reflected in men's feelings. Men seem to be suffering grievances or perceptions of injustice of their own. A new breed of "angry white men" believe that everyone has rights except them (Estrich 1994). Men are angry not only because they have lost ground but also because they are tired of being blamed for all of women's troubles. "The American man wants his manhood back," says Sam Allis in an article titled, "What Do Men Really Want?" (1990). One would predict high levels of anger among men as well as women, although men may well have a different set of grievances.

The question is not only whether men and women are angry, but also how they respond to each other's anger. Gergen and Gergen (1988) found that acceptance of blame was the most frequent response to another person's anger; in such cases, the target of the anger apologized and felt remorse. In the second most frequent response, the target reframed the incident so that it seemed less blameworthy or bad ("I did it only because I thought it would help"). In the least frequent response, the target rejected the implication of the other person's anger and became angry in return. This third response leads most easily to an escalation of hostilities on both sides, and I believe it has become more common.

Many widespread structural changes and cultural emphases associated with postindustrial society contribute to the conflict, frustrations, anger, and sometimes aggression between the sexes. Although such an analysis makes the possible sources of anger and hostility more understandable, it does not reveal how angry women and men actually are, what women and men perceive to be the most important sources of gender anger, how they perceive each other, or how they express or deal with anger. For this understanding, one must listen to the voices of the women and men themselves. This book seeks to fill this gap in our knowledge.

Chapter 3

Anger

Much of what we do and how we do it is influenced by emotions and
the conditions that generate them. (Lazarus 1991)

Understanding our emotional selves, especially in regard to potentially negative
emotions such as anger, is increasingly seen as an important endeavor. Several
recent books, such as Harriet Lerner's *The Dance of Anger* (1985), *When Anger
Kills* (1993) by Redford and Virginia Williams, and *Anger in the Workplace*
(1994) by Seth Allcorn, exemplify this concern. Daniel Goleman's *Emotional
Intelligence* (1995) argues that we have given too much importance to the kind of
intelligence that is measured by IQ and not enough to the factors that allow us to
function in the emotional realm. Emotional intelligence (EQ) comprises self-
awareness, impulse control, persistence, self-motivation, empathy, and social
deftness, all of them critical to making relationships with others work in both the
private and public realms. Goleman's book features groundbreaking research on
brain circuitry by Joseph LeDoux, a neuroscientist at the Center for Neural Science
at New York University, whose work explains why and how our rational selves
can be quickly and completely overcome by angry impulse. Others have urged us
to pay more attention to the emotions, "the deep, passionate relationship
experiences" (both positive and negative), as Aron and Aron (cited by Rook 1995)
put it. These emotional experiences are perceived to be crucial for our personal
and social well-being.

Although the emotions were given some attention by classic theorists
such as Durkheim, Simmel, Weber, and (later) Homans, this area did not receive
much notice until the 1970s and 1980s (Kemper 1978). Until then, sociology and
psychology had stressed the importance of cognition rather than emotion (Smith-
Lovin 1989). According to Carroll Izard (1991), the sociology of emotion is just
coming of age. Social scientists finally have recognized that feelings lie at the

center of human experience and adaptation (Lazarus 1991). Sociologists are challenging the popular view of emotions, which conceptualizes them as private, biological, or psychological phenomena, and instead emphasize their social and contextual nature. Most of the work in this area has been done at the micro- or sociopsychological level of analysis rather than at the macro- or structural-cultural level (Thoits 1989).

The traditional view depicted emotions as simple, involuntary, and purely affective states, but today most scholars conceive of emotions as socially constructed. From this perspective, emotions can be regarded as belief systems or schemas that guide the appraisal of situations, the organization of responses, and the self-monitoring or interpretation of behavior. Emotional schemas are the internal representations of social norms or rules (Averill 1986). Emotions are always interpersonal or relational; one must take into account the person and the situation. As Carole Tavris (1989) states, angry episodes are social events; the meaning comes from the social relationship of the participants.

THE IMPORTANCE OF ANGER IN HUMAN RELATIONSHIPS

Anger is basic to our human selves. A complex emotional experience (Thomas 1993) and one of the most frequently encountered emotions (Averill 1993), it is a major difficulty in all human relationships. As Silvin Tomkins (1991) puts it, anger is the most urgent of all affects and the most problematic in social interactions.

Most of us take anger for granted, although we usually fear it in ourselves and in others. Although anger "may be the most forbidden of emotions" (Allcorn 1994, xii), scholars and nonscholars alike increasingly believe that we cannot afford to ignore it and that we should respect rather than fear it. It is difficult to develop a positive attitude toward anger because we live in a society that strongly disapproves of this emotion (Pollak and Thoits 1989). "Anger has a bad rap," says Joy Browne in her newsletter (1997). It is seen as one of the "deadly sins," as dangerous and antisocial. However, she claims, it is *unexpressed* anger that is the culprit; expressed anger (as long as it is not violent) is necessary in our daily lives. Carol and Peter Stearns (1986) view the restraint of anger as one of the significant themes in American culture and claim this has been normative for almost two hundred years. Most children learn early in life that anger is bad and dangerous, that they should not feel it at all or should learn not to express it (at least directly), and that they should avoid people who are angry. Gayle Denham and Kaye Bultemeier quote a passage from Duerk's *Circle of Stones: Woman's Journey to Herself*, which asks:

How might it have been different for you, if, early in your life, the first time you as a tiny child felt your anger coming together inside yourself, someone, a parent or grandparent, or older sister or brother, had said, "Bravo! Yes, that's it! You're feeling it!" If, the first time you had experienced that sharp awareness of ego of "me, I'm me, not you"...you had been received and hugged and affirmed, instead of shamed and isolated. (1993, 68)

Perhaps if we grew up with a more positive perspective of anger, it would tend to be productive rather than destructive. Yet despite its potential to hurt and destroy, anger serves important social functions; otherwise, as James Averill (1982) has said, it would not have been an essential feature of Western civilization for over 2,500 years.

According to Averill (1982), anger is primarily an interpersonal emotion and is more likely to be associated with love than with hate. Thus, a person is more likely to become angry toward loved ones and friends than toward strangers and disliked others. One reason is that our contact with loved ones is close and continual, and this increases the chance of a provocation; more time is spent at risk. Also, we tend to be less inhibited in our expression and experience of anger with those we care about. In addition, the transgressions committed by those we care about tend to be more distressing as well as cumulative. Finally, we usually feel a stronger motivation to make loved ones change their ways.

Scholars have offered many explanations for anger. Tavris (1989) says that anger is ultimately an empathic message: "Pay attention to me"; "I don't like what you're doing"; "Restore my dignity and pride"; "Danger ahead"; "Give me justice." Averill (1993) believes that the proper goal of anger is to correct a perceived wrong rather than to hurt the target. Melvyn Fein (1993) views anger as a sign of something gone wrong—a warning that stressors are exceeding our resources, our experience is too much or too punishing, our rights and values are being compromised, others are doing too much or too little for us. The basic purpose of anger is to influence others. Another function, according to Fein, is to answer the anger of others or "counter-anger," which establishes independence and respect by sending the message, "I'm a person to be reckoned with." It is important, says Fein, to express anger so that the offending party has an opportunity to make necessary changes. As a motivator for change, according to Izard (1991), anger mobilizes energy and guides mental and physical activity. Such energy is usually needed for psychological defense; it provides the firmness and determination that keep us from being bullied.

Communicating anger often has the constructive function of generating solutions to interpersonal problems. Unless perceptions of unfairness or injustice are shared, there is little or no chance of resolving the problem. It is unclear how regularly people share their feelings of anger. In her study of 535 healthy women ages twenty-five to sixty-six, Sandra Thomas (1993) reports that only 9.6 percent spoke directly to the person with whom they were angry.

Research by Averill (1983) shows that most of his sample of college students who had been targets of anger said they understood their own faults more clearly after the expression of anger. The students claimed that their relationships with the other person were often strengthened as a result of the anger episode. Baumeister, Stillwell, and Wotman (1990), however, found that the communication of a grievance damaged relationships. They speculate that the disagreements in their sample were more severe than in Averill's. Displays of anger may be regarded by others as accusatory, insulting, or disruptive, and thus may be the first steps in an escalating cycle of conflict between individuals (Novaco 1976).

Anger is considered a positive force in individuals' lives when it is used to correct a situation, restore equity, or prevent a recurrence of harm. It is destructive when used to inflict injury or pain or achieve selfish ends (Averill 1993). Anger must be managed, says Fein (1993), and to be managed it must be understood. When anger is understood properly, it is neither something loathsome to be hidden nor something to be displayed proudly; it is neither evil nor sacrosanct. It should facilitate the achievement of important personal or social goals; it should be used as a tool for living. Anger can be a sign of respect for a loved person or a sign of self-love or self-respect. It becomes a problem when it goes out of control and causes injury to others when it is turned inward and inflicts damage on the self or when it is so ineffectual that it does not achieve the goal it is intended to serve. Fein calls out-of-control anger, overcontrolled anger, and ineffectual anger the "troika of infamy." People who cannot get angry or cannot do so effectively are at a disadvantage because they lose the possibility of equal relationships and may not meet certain needs. How we manage anger has powerful and potentially dangerous implications for our private lives and our social policies. It affects the entire web of our social relations (Tavris 1989).

Because the goal of anger is to eliminate frustrations or counteract external threats, one or the other of these outcomes must occur if the angry person is to stop feeling angry. Merely expressing anger, hurting someone, or suppressing anger is not sufficient (Fein 1993). The intensity of anger communicates the degree of unjust harm experienced by the angered party. Anger functions to draw the other person's attention to the issues of concern to the angered person. It indicates a commitment to resolving the grievance (Tedeschi and Nesler 1993). If the grievance is not resolved, the angered person awaits a triggering event to release justice-restoring behavior.

Influencing others in ways that allow us to get what we want without hurting someone else is "an extraordinarily convoluted process" (Fein 1993). The outcome depends on what is wanted, what kind of resources one has, and who the opponent is. Fein (1993) observes that one of the most difficult situations is one in which the interacting parties are "locked into patterns of mutual dependency and obligation." Spouses or intimate others, however, have one advantage: their motivation to work things out is greater than usual because so much is invested in continuing the relationship.

Sometimes anger is accompanied by feelings of helplessness or by an inability to cope. It does not thrive in situations where response options are either too limited or too abundant. When no responses are viable, a threat that would usually lead to anger leads instead to fear or depression. If the person can deal easily with the situation, it can be viewed merely as a minor nuisance or an annoyance. "Anger is an escalated response"; it arises when other efforts to cope have failed or are not considered likely to lead to success (Averill 1982, 247).

The current situation between women and men seems conducive to generating anger. Many individuals seem to feel that they are being treated unfairly by the other sex. Unlike women in the past, many women today believe that they have options. Increased job opportunities and greater tolerance for alternative lifestyles make it easier for women to live on their own or with other women. The kind of anger that men and women are feeling is not clear. Is it the "counter-anger" that Fein describes? Is it the kind of anger that says, "Pay attention to me"? Is it the kind that says, "Give me justice"? As Fein pointed out, the dynamics of anger grow more complex when people are in a relationship of dependence and obligation, as are women and men.

DEFINITIONS AND DISTINCTIONS

In this book I focus on anger and gender relations. Although *anger* is a common word and most of us can easily recognize anger in ourselves or in others, defining this term is not simple. Siegel (1986) points out that operational definitions of anger vary widely across studies, making it difficult to compare the results.

According to Edmunds and Kendrick (1980), there is no unified definition of anger. Often, in fact, there is no explicit definition of anger. Fein (1993), for example, wrote a whole book (and an excellent one) on anger management without offering a precise definition. He discusses positive and negative functions of anger, offers interesting theoretical views on anger, and makes many useful suggestions for how to live with anger, but provides no definition. The picture is complicated by researchers who use words such as *anger*, *hostility*, and *aggression* interchangeably.

I view anger and hostility as two separate, though related, concepts. Thomas's distinction is useful. She defines anger as a "strong feeling of distress or displeasure in response to a specific provocation of some kind" (1993, 13), such as a threat, injury, or injustice. Hostility, she says, "implies a more pervasive and enduring antagonistic mental attitude" (13). Arnold Buss (1961) also believes that hostility implies a negative evaluation of people and events and that hostile people hold on to past attacks, rejections, and deprivations. Research by James Tedeschi and Richard Felson (1994) indicates that when people interpret another person's behavior as hostile, they are likely to feel upset and to retaliate. Some scholars, such as Kaufman (1970, cited by Edmunds and Kendrick 1980), describe hostility as a habitual propensity for disliking others, wishing them harm, or acting aggressively toward them; this definition blurs the distinction between hostility and aggression. Others, such as Izard (1991), believe that hostility involves wishing others harm, embarrassment, or defeat but does not include verbal or physical activity. His phrase "the hostility triad" is an attempt to capture the fact that situations that elicit anger tend to elicit disgust and contempt as well.

Hostility seems to subsume anger: If I'm hostile, I will probably feel anger, but I may be angry and not be hostile. John Barefoot's (1992) definition of hostility incorporates three components—cognitive, affective, and behavioral—that are useful in visualizing the relationship of hostility, anger, and aggression. The cognitive component consists of negative beliefs about others ("Most women lie to get ahead"); these beliefs increase the likelihood that others' behavior will be interpreted as antagonistic or threatening and will help to justify the hostile person's own negative behavior toward others. The affective component includes emotional states such as anger, resentment, disgust, and contempt. Such states tend to be accompanied by physiological activity. The behavioral component includes aggression, both verbal and nonverbal, as well as other forms of antagonistic behavior. Barefoot points out that these three components covary but do not always occur together. He warns that the use of self-report measures threatens the validity of measures of hostility primarily because subjects feel pressure to give socially desirable answers. This bias is especially strong in the case of hostility because hostility is valued negatively in our society. Also, the most hostile subjects may be more likely than the more trusting individuals to give distorted responses.

Many other words refer to related negative feelings. Richard Lazarus (1991), for example, says that a large number of terms "fall within the emotion family of anger" (227). In this family he lists *rage, outrage, fury, wrath, ferocity, indignation, irritation, annoyance,* and *hatred.* One could add *resentment, disgust,* and *contempt* as well. Some of these terms represent varying intensities of the same feeling, but others signify different feelings. As an example, Lazarus states that *outrage* implies having been wronged, whereas *rage* does not. (For an extended discussion on the differences between anger and annoyance, see Averill 1982, chapter 11.)

Various researchers offer their analysis of the components and themes associated with anger. Izard (1991) says that the object of an emotion is one of its strongest defining traits and that the object usually includes three aspects: the instigation, the target, and the aim or objective. In the case of anger, the instigation is a perceived wrong; the aim is the correction of the wrong; the target is another human being or some other entity, such as the self or an institution, that can be held responsible.

In an attempt to distinguish among emotions, Lazarus (1991) offers a "relational theme" for anger. He states that a "demeaning offense against me and mine is the best shorthand description of the provocation to adult human anger" (222). Lazarus believes that all anger situations involve a threat to ego identity. An emotion (any emotion) comes into existence only if "goal relevance" is present—that is, if the individual has a personal stake in the encounter. If the interaction is inconsistent with what the person wants, "goal incongruence" exists, and a negative (as opposed to a positive) emotion is generated.

Goal relevance, goal incongruence, and threat to ego identity lay the foundation for anger, but several "secondary appraisal" components must be present in order to cause anger rather than other negative emotions. First, anger occurs only if a specific type of ego involvement, the assault of one's self- or social esteem, is activated. If other aspects of one's ego identity are threatened, other emotions arise, such as anxiety, guilt, shame, or envy.

A second key element is blame, which concerns who, if anyone, is held accountable for damage or threat to our identity. If we hold ourselves accountable, we may experience anger, guilt, or shame. If nobody is held accountable, we probably experience sadness. Anger could occur if the direction of accountability is external and if we attribute control to the other person or object: "If the people who frustrated us are not thought to be in control of their actions, no blame can logically be assigned to them" (Lazarus 1991, 223). Averill (1983) studied college students' memories of what made them feel angry. Typically they recalled events that they described as voluntary and unjustified or as harmful and avoidable. Thus, attributing blame and responsibility to others is a critical process in creating angry feelings. Lazarus notes that it may very difficult to judge who, if anyone, should properly be blamed because one can assign accountability and control, and thus place blame, at many levels. In a more complex society, the judgment is even more difficult because there are more potential targets.

A third variable that influences what emotion is generated is "coping potential." Anger, as opposed to fear or anxiety, results when the person perceives that the offense is handled most effectively by attack. Finally, Lazarus says that we evaluate the environmental response to attack. If "future expectancy" is positive, then anger is facilitated.

According to Lazarus, a particular goal must be frustrated to cause anger: the preservation or enhancement of ego identity. Not all scholars agree with Lazarus. Berkowitz (1989), for example, takes the position that anger is not restricted to situations in which one's personal or social identity is devalued. He claims that *any* frustration of an expected gratification is sufficient, but this seems to be a minority position.

In his research on motives from the perspective of the angry person, Averill (1982) identifies three kinds of anger: malevolent, constructive, and fractious. Malevolent anger is characterized by motives such as "to express dislike," "to break off a relationship," and "to gain revenge." Constructive anger is represented by feelings such as "to strengthen the relationship," "to assert authority," and "to get the other to do something for you." Averill describes this kind of anger as a "complex blend of self-centered and altruistic motives" (179). The third type, fractious anger, involves "letting off steam." Averill cautions that together the three kinds of anger account for only 47 percent of the variance; this finding suggests a considerable amount of variability in the patterns of motivation. Further analyses by Averill show that the nature of the target and the relationship to the target affect the motivation to some extent. Thus, for example, the motive "to get even for past wrongs" was reported most frequently when the target was disliked rather than liked.

One must also distinguish between internal feelings of anger and expressions of anger. One can display anger whether one feels it or not; conversely, one can act calm and collected and yet be very angry.

In my research, I have used the phrase *gender hostility* primarily because it slides off the tongue more easily than *gender anger*. In this book, however, I explore anger. My sense is that women and men mostly feel anger, either major or minor, toward each other. Hostility implies a seething, spiteful, hateful, vengeful antagonism that most of us cannot sustain. Hostility colors one's view of everything, something like wearing mud-colored glasses, while anger allows negative feeling to wane. Hostility implies revenge and gaining satisfaction from the other's downfall or bad fortune; in contrast, the goal of anger is to overcome some frustration or to right a perceived wrong. Anger dissipates once the other person apologizes, but it is not clear how hostility is decreased. Hostility is often conceptualized so as to appear to be a permanent, underlying disposition (Check 1988). If this is the case, changes in situation or attitude are unlikely to decrease hostile feelings.

ANGER AND AGGRESSION

Researchers typically have not separated the expression of anger from aggression. Frequently they lump these concepts together because they believe that anger often causes aggression (Clark 1992; Zillman 1979). Although some research indicates that anger is a common precursor to aggression (Baron 1977), one can be angry or hostile without engaging in overt acts of aggression, and one can be aggressive without feeling angry or hostile (Zillman 1979). Averill provides an apt analogy to the relationship between anger and aggression: "The availability of a blueprint does not cause the building to be constructed, but it does make construction easier. Anger no more causes aggression than a blueprint causes the construction of a building" (1993, 188–89).

Izard, like Averill, believes that although hostile and angry feelings may increase the likelihood of aggression, they are not invariably connected. In a study of causes and consequences of anger in college students and community residents, Averill (1983) found that only 10 percent of 160 anger experiences resulted in physical aggression or punishment, and 49 percent in verbal aggression. Nonaggressive responses, such as talking about the incident, occurred in 60 percent of the incidents.

When distinctions are made, researchers usually define aggression as an actual physical or verbal attack, whereas anger refers to a strong feeling of distress (Thomas 1993). Some researchers, such as Izard (1991), believe that intention to harm is part of the physical or psychological action of aggression.

Because anger is potentially so constructive, we cannot afford to leave it alone, to not teach others ways to deal with it constructively. Only then can it realize its positive functions: to serve as a warning, energize us for action, motivate us to understand others' feelings, and work toward justice.

Chapter 4

Correlates of Gender and Anger

[Gender is one] of the three central themes out of which we fashion the
meaning of our lives. (Kimmel and Messner 1989)

Popular stereotypes typically do not associate females with the direct expression of
anger. Brody and Hall (1993) reviewed research on gender and emotion and
found that people very clearly see females as more expressive than males when it
comes to many emotions, but not in regard to anger, which was associated with
males. They cite studies that indicate the consistency of such beliefs; people from
various socioeconomic and age backgrounds share the belief that anger is
expressed more often and more intensely by males. Cultural norms encourage or
at least allow males to respond angrily when provoked; cultural definitions of
femininity make it difficult for females to be openly hostile or angry. If women
fail to restrain their anger, they tend to be viewed as emotional or hysterical
(Crawford and Kippax 1992). These assumptions are reflected in the research
literature, which focuses primarily on male-to-male or male-to-female hostility and
aggression, rather than hostility and aggression on the part of females directed at
either at men or other women.

This double standard is beginning to erode. Some observers believe that
women can be more aggressive and assertive today, although they are still subject
to more limits than men (Black 1990). Francesca Cancian and Steven Gordon
(1988) document a normative shift in the twentieth century, which actually
encourages women today to express emotions such as anger. Their research linked
marital emotion norms to political and cultural events and found that in periods of
social upheaval, women are encouraged to be more open with their anger.

Research presents mixed findings in regard to gender and various measures
of anger and hostility. For self-reported hostility, paper-and-pencil measures such
as the Buss-Durkee Hostility Inventory have not revealed sex differences. Barefoot

et al. (1991), using a large national sample, found that men outscored women on cynical hostility regardless of age. James Check and Neil Malamuth (1985) assessed hostility in Canadian women and men and found that the men's average score was slightly higher than the women's (8.79 versus 7.57). When men and women were asked to keep track of specific anger experiences, Campbell (1993) found no significant differences in the frequency of such experiences: over a one-week period, men reported that they became angry between six and seven times, and women between five and six times.

Tavris (1989) examined sex differences in anger and found no differences in how anger is experienced, how it is expressed, how well it is identified, or what categories of things arouse anger. She believes, however, that although women do not feel anger any less strongly than men, they are less likely to express it because of the costs associated with their lower social status. Tavris points out that men and women become angry about the same categories of offenses, such as condescending treatment, injustice, and attacks on self-esteem, but they often disagree about what they *consider* to be condescending treatment, injustice, or attack. Frodi and Macaulay (1977) found that both women and men were angered by condescending treatment: women regardless of the provoker's sex and men by a superior attitude on the part of a female. Men were more angered than women by physical and verbal aggression on the part of another male.

Brody and Hall (1993) reviewed studies showing that there are fairly clear-cut differences in regard to positive emotions (with women experiencing and expressing them more), but in regard to negative emotions, especially anger, the findings are less consistent. Females were more likely to feel and express "intropunitive" emotions (such as shame, sadness, and guilt), and men were more likely to feel and express "outward directed" emotions (such as contempt). However, for anger, differences between the sexes are often very small or males are more angry than females. Kopper and Epperson (1991) looked at the relationship between sex and sex role identity on anger expression and found sex not to be an important factor in the expression or suppression of anger (however, sex role identity was).

Some research finds more anger on the part of females. The review article by Brody and Hall (1993) cites research by Brody that found more anger on the part of women toward imaginary male protagonists. Mirowsky and Ross (1995) investigated whether women's greater distress accounts are a function of women's greater expressiveness (they are not) or whether they truly experience more distress (they do). In the process of their work they found that females experience various feelings, including anger, more often than males. Reiser (1994) explored respondents' feelings of anger toward the other sex using a random sample of North Carolina residents and found a significant sex difference, with female respondents reporting greater anger than male respondents. Conger et al. (1993, cited by Miroswky and Ross 1995) surveyed 451 married couples who lived in the rural Midwest and found that the women reported significantly greater levels of marital hostility than the men.

Men tend to be targets of anger or aggression more often than women. Averill (1982) found, however, that the target's sex varied, depending on the type of relationship between the angry person and the target. In a love relationship, men became angry at women, and women became angry at men. When angry episodes involved someone who was well liked and well known, same-sexed dyads were most common; men became angry more often at other men and women at other women. Male targets outnumbered female targets primarily in the "acquaintance" and "stranger" categories. Averill also found that episodes of anger described by women were rated as more intense and further out of proportion to the precipitating incident than those described by men; more women than men said they wanted to talk over the anger incident with the instigator; the women reported crying more often than the men; and the women reported greater tension. In regard to another person's anger, Averill (1982) found that the women, more often than the men, reacted with hurt feelings, while the men, more often than the women, reacted with defiance. The women in the sample were more likely to believe that the instigation violated a personal expectation or wish on the angry person's part. They felt that the other person's anger was unnecessarily intense.

In contrast to researchers such as Averill and Tavris, who believe that women and men are much more alike than different in regard to anger, Crawford and Kippax (1992) conclude that important differences exist primarily because structured patterns of dominance create different cultures for men and for women. These authors recognize that standards of emotional appropriateness may be applied differently to women and to men, not only because of sex but also because of a power-status difference (Shields 1987). The key mediating variable is differential power. Thus, for women, anger is the expression of frustration and powerlessness; it is a response to feelings of injustice and unfairness. Women cry much more often than men in anger situations, according to Crawford and Kippax (1992), because when women become frustrated, they hold in their frustration for a long time and finally lose control in an explosive fashion. Men have less reason to feel powerless and therefore experience less anger due to powerlessness and frustration. Men don't feel victimized; they use anger as a way to ensure their power. Their anger derives from a sense that their rights, property, or authority have been challenged in some way. Men's anger disappears quickly if they deflect the challenge or threat successfully, whereas women tend to feel overwhelmed and stressed by angry or hostile actions.

Similar themes are stated by Anne Campbell (1993) and by Campbell and Muncer (1987). Campbell (1993) claims that men and women have different social representations of anger as well as of aggression; women's representation is "expressive" and men's is "instrumental." Social representation refers to everyday theories or explanations of causes of events as well as to our overall notion of anger. It includes our interpretations of an anger incident, our emotional responses, and what we actually do when angry. These representations are influential in shaping our behavior. For example, if I believe that hitting someone shows a loss of self-control, I will be more likely to hit someone in private than in public.

Campbell and Muncer (1987) analyzed interactions in a group of friends who engaged informally in social talk in same-sex groups. They reported some similarities and several differences between male and female groups. For both sexes, most of the anger episodes were concerned with issues of personal integrity. Among women, however, the second most common reason for anger was jealousy, while men were divided between physical harm and others' incompetence. The women more often discussed spouse-lover episodes; the men more often discussed friend-acquaintance episodes. This difference in topics would account for some of the differences in findings. The women commonly raised issues relating to tension between anger and self-control; they wanted to maintain self-control but were frustrated by not expressing their feelings. They felt themselves to be in a no-win situation. The women displayed different responses to this tension. Sometimes they did nothing, which made them feel good because it was a sign of self-control, but it also made them feel powerless and regretful. Sometimes they broke down and cried; this reaction usually made them feel bad because it cast them in the role of a child or a manipulator. Sometimes they reacted aggressively; this response made them feel bad because of fear that they would be viewed as bitchy, fear of their own anger, or fear of rejection.

Men did not seem to experience this dilemma. They did not interpret the issue as a matter of self-control. For men, the issue was one of social management; they expressed concern about the propriety of anger and aggression in different settings and with different opponents. Men faced a no-lose situation.

An important article by La France and Banaji (1992) further delineates the complexity of the gender-emotion relationship. These authors believe that reality is distorted by widespread, deeply held beliefs of gender differences in emotionality. They claim that such differences in emotionality could be due to the way it is measured. The authors discuss three ways of measuring emotional states: self-report, nonverbal expressivity, and physiological indicators. The most common modality through which emotions manifest themselves is self-report. According to their review of literature in the 1980s, "Females will report being more emotional than males when the measure is direct rather than indirect, when the self-reported emotion is potentially perceptible by others rather than privately experienced, when the context is interpersonal rather than impersonal, and when global rather than discrete emotion is examined" (188). They hypothesize that conformity to prescribed gender roles plays an important role in the findings, especially when respondents are asked about general rather than specific emotions, in general rather than particular contexts.

My own work documents high levels of anger on the part of women and men in reference to various issues. Although I found significant sex differences they did not emerge in all situations. My exploratory study in 1993 investigated the attitudes of a convenience sample of college students in introductory level sociology classes at a large, southern university. Students reported on the extent of resentful feelings toward the other sex as well as the perceived level of resentment toward members of their own sex. Two open-ended questions explored sources of resentment: what made respondents feel resentful toward the other sex and their perceptions of what made the other sex feel resentful toward their own sex. The results showed different patterns for males and females, with many more women feeling resentful than men. For example, 38 percent of the males said they feel resentment toward women either "sometimes" or "a lot," while 63 percent of the women felt resentment toward men at those levels. A sex difference was also found for perceptions of others' levels of resentment with 61 percent of the females and 87 percent of the males believing that the other sex resents members of their own sex either "sometimes" or "a lot." Clearly, fewer women sense resentment from men than men do from women.

Responses to the open-ended questions indicated that women and men share similar perceptions as to sources of anger. Female respondents think that males resent women who challenge men's dominance, who receive unfair advantages, and who have negative personal attributes (dishonesty). Males said that they resent women who exhibit negative personal attributes (bitching, being cold) and have unfair advantages. Interestingly, men did not complain as much about "uppity women" as females thought they would. Male respondents felt that women resent men who treat women as inferiors, who have negative personal attributes, who are sexually aggressive, and when men receive unfair advantages. Female respondents said they resent men because they treat women as inferiors, aggress against them sexually, have negative personal attributes, enjoy unfair advantages, and don't have to suffer physical hardships like pregnancy and menstruation. My 1995 study, using a random sample of students, focused on their opinions and levels of anger in the areas of sexuality, work, and power, as well as toward general male-female relationships. Over half of the female respondents and almost half of the male respondents agreed that the way the other sex treated them today made them angry. Each of the specific topic questions was framed so that they applied to females and males. Statistically significant differences based on sex were found for each of the attitude items. More females than males saw men as always being preoccupied with sex and more males than females believed that women use sex as a way to manipulate men. Males were less likely than females to believe that men have greater job opportunities and rewards than women. More males than females see women as having greater job opportunities in the labor force. More females than males agree that men try to control women and more males than females see women as trying to dominate men. It is interesting to note that the statements dealing with dominance or power tapped the highest levels of anger for both sexes.

An interesting pattern emerged in regard to feelings of anger. Whenever a statement referred to male behavior or privilege, males and females differed significantly in their expressed anger. However, whenever female behavior or privilege was the referent, there were no significant differences in anger between women and men. For example, many more females than males were angry about men trying to control women, but when it came to women trying to control men, there was no sex difference in anger. One would have expected that relatively few females would say they are angry about aspects of female behavior or, conversely, that more males would be angry over female behavior than females. It appears that a different anger standard exists for judging men's behavior since women's behavior elicits the same anger feelings. This pattern extended to general male-female relationships as well. Twice as many women (69.2 percent) as men (29.6 percent) agreed that "the way men treat women today makes me angry," but there was no sex difference for the way women treat men today (close to 50 percent of both women and men said this made them angry).

In terms of implications for future male-female relations, this study yielded a mixed picture. On the one hand, the fact that so many women and men were angry about the way the other sex treated them and the lack of congruence between men's and women's perceptions on some of the topics portends more tension and conflict in the future. On the other hand, the fact that over half of the men in this sample say it makes them angry when "men act like they have the right to control women" and when men focus too much on sex may be a sign of change in a more egalitarian direction.

My third study (unpublished) examined attitudes and feelings of anger in regard to five potentially conflictual issues in male-female relationships using a random sample of over 1000 individuals from forty-one Eastern North Carolina counties. The five issues were job opportunities and rewards, housework, dominance, sexual relations, and attempts to understand each other. Respondents' level of agreement in reference to these issues was measured, as were their feelings of anger in regard to these issues. This provided a context for interpreting the anger. For example, the majority of female respondents may indicate they are angry when men "don't do their share of the housework," but what if only 8 percent of these women believe that men don't do their fair share? Thus, each of the five areas of conflict was broken down into parallel sets of questions, with one asking for the level of agreement and the other for the degree of anger associated with a particular issue. Each issue focused on both males and females (see Table 1).

As in the previous study, two questions tapping a general or overall sense of anger were included. This study also asked for respondents' estimates of anger frequency. They were asked to assess how often they felt angry toward members of the other sex, how often they thought members of the other sex felt angry toward themselves ("personalized anger"), how often members of their own sex felt angry toward members of the other sex, and how often they thought members of the other sex felt angry toward members of their own sex ("generalized anger"). Another question asked respondents to judge whether relations between men and women today are better, worse, or about the same as ten years ago.

Again, women and men shared a single standard for judging women's behavior but a double standard for men's behavior. Results show a clear-cut sex difference in all instances where men are the referent, with women feeling greater anger than men. The fact that more than half of the women were angry for each of these items (specific or general) shows that we are talking about substantial numbers of women. The highest percentages were associated with statements referring to dominance and understanding. Such high levels of anger assume even

Table 1
Gender Role Attitudes and Perceptions of Anger (by Percent Who Agree)

		Female	Male	P
1.	Men typically have greater job opportunities and rewards than women.	79.9	69.2	.000
2.	It makes me angry when men have greater job opportunities and rewards than women.	62.0	38.4	.000
3.	Women typically have greater job opportunities and rewards than men.	8.7	15.9	.000
4.	It makes me angry when women have greater job opportunities and rewards than men.	18.5	16.3	.598
5.	Men typically don't do their share of work around the house.	69.4	51.8	.000
6.	It makes me angry when men don't do their share of work around the house.	75.1	45.6	.000
7.	Women typically don't do their share of work around the house.	15.6	13.2	.075
8.	It makes me angry when women don't do their share of work around the house.	58.8	53.6	.462
9.	Men typically act like they have the right to tell women what to do.	66.1	48.5	.000
10.	It makes me angry when men act like they have the right to tell women what to do.	84.3	63.9	.000
11.	Women typically act like they have the right to tell men what to do.	33.8	40.2	.224
12.	It makes me angry when women act like they have the right to men what to do.	61.3	63.2	.197
13.	When it comes to sexual relations, men really don't care about women's feelings.	38.2	23.3	.000

Table 1 (Continued)
Gender Role Attitudes and Perceptions of Anger (by Percent Who Agree)

		Female	Male	P
14.	It makes me angry when men don't care about women's feelings when it comes to sexual relations.	78.7	65.1	.000
15.	When it comes to sexual relations, women really don't care about men's feelings.	17.2	15.8	.309
16.	It makes me angry when women don't care about men's feelings when it comes to sexual relations.	59.4	60.5	.030
17.	Men don't try to understand women.	55.6	41.7	.000
18.	It makes me angry when men don't try to understand women.	81.2	59.5	.000
19.	Women don't try to understand men.	39.0	35.3	.726
20.	It makes me angry when women don't try to understand men.	68.3	61.6	.177
21.	The way men treat women today makes me angry.	61.3	50.8	.011
22.	The way women treat men today makes me angry.	51.8	48.4	.482

more significance given the largely rural and conservative nature of the sample. When female behavior was the referent, men achieved levels of 50 percent or more with all issues except job opportunities and rewards. The highest proportion of angry men was found in reference to women acting as if they have the right to tell men what to do (dominance). This echoes the women's sentiments; clearly, neither sex likes to be dominated by the other.

When women's behavior was the referent, the sex difference disappeared. Men were not more angry than women when it came to negative things that women do to men, or women were just as angry at their own sex for doing something wrong to men as men were angry at women. It is not clear why women and men share a single standard for women's behavior but a double standard for men's behavior. One explanation may be that women have internalized new, nonsexist expectations (men are not supposed to dominate women) and thus get angry when men don't live up to them. Men may be more ambivalent about adopting norms that take away some of their traditional power and privilege. This would make them less angry about their own sexist behavior. Women and men may see eye to eye in regard to women's behavior since it is easy for women to condemn sexist, unfair behavior in either sex and it is easier for men to get frustrated when women are stepping out of their traditional role or are not doing what they're supposed to (such as staying home and taking care of the house and children). Part of the explanation may have to do with the content of the items. The women should not give up traditional behavior (for example, they should not give up doing housework, but simply should do no more than their share) unlike the men, who *should* give up traditional behaviors, like telling women what to do. Nor should the women adopt traditional male behavior (telling men what to do). It may be that men and women are in greater agreement on the new norms for females, and thus we find no sex differences on all issues dealing with females. All the male-oriented items referred to situations that are now "politically incorrect" (damaging to women), and thus one would expect women and men to be equally angry, but perhaps men still believe that such behaviors and attitudes are acceptable—indeed, consistent with a masculine orientation. It may be that women are applying the same standards of fairness to their own behavior as well as to men's, and thus they get just as angry when members of their own sex are politically incorrect.

The responses of males to male behavior showed that large proportions (one-third or more) of the respondents said they were angry when men have greater job opportunities, don't do their share around the house, act like they have the right to tell women what to do, don't care about women's sexual feelings, don't try to understand women, and about the way men treat women today. Men not caring about women's feelings when it comes to sexual relations drew the highest proportion of angry men; fully 65 percent of the male respondents said this situation made them angry. These findings indicate that significant proportions of men are rejecting traditional male stereotypes and are judging behavior according to more equalitarian, relationship-oriented standards.

Smucker et al. (1993) say that "anger is a personal evaluation of the significance of an incident that conflicts with our values or view of the world." If we accept that emotion discloses value, it appears (based on the highest proportions) that men feel most strongly about men and women trying to dominate each other, not caring about each other's sexual feelings, and not trying to understand each other. Women also value relationships where men and women don't dominate each other, care about each other's sexual feelings, and try to understand each other; in addition, women seem to have a greater investment in tangible conditions such as sharing housework and access to equal job opportunities.

Another kind of double standard seems to exist for "personalized" and "generalized" perceptions of how often anger occurs (see Table 2). When asked how often the other sex felt angry toward themselves personally, relatively few (13.5 percent of females and 12.1 percent of males) respondents said either "always" or "often." However, when judging how often members of the other sex felt angry toward members of their own sex, the proportion answering "always" or "often" was much higher (39.4 percent of females and 30.1 percent of males). The same pattern held for anger projected at others. Small numbers of respondents (9.6 percent of females and 5.9 percent of males) admitted to feeling personally angry toward members of the other sex, but many more respondents (39.7 percent of females and 23.7 percent of males) claimed that members of their own sex felt angry toward the other sex. The general theme is "I don't get angry at others and they don't get angry at me personally, but others give and receive a lot of anger."

Table 2
Perceptions of Personalized Anger: Percentage
Answering "Always" or "Often"

	Female	Male	P
How often do you feel angry towards members of the opposite sex?	9.6	5.9	.000
How often do you think members of the opposite sex feel angry toward you?	13.5	12.1	.266

Women were more likely than men to attribute high levels of anger on part of themselves and others toward men and on the part of men toward women (see Table 3) For example, almost 40 percent of female respondents (compared to 30 percent of male respondents) thought that women were either "always" or "often" angry toward men and 40 percent of females (compared to 25 percent of males) thought that men were "always" or "often" angry toward women.   Male respondents were less likely to report anger toward others, either on behalf of themselves or their sex, and also were less likely to perceive anger toward their own sex.   Male and female respondents did not differ significantly in their perceptions of how often members of the opposite sex were angry toward themselves personally.   This study also documents high levels of anger in reference to specific issues and for relations between women and men in general; half of the female respondents and close to half of the male respondents judged relations between women and men as being worse today than ten years ago.

The research points to the need for continued sensitivity to differences based on sex. The patterns are not always consistent. Sex differences may emerge or disappear depending on the issue, the point of reference, or the specificity of the items. Both may become angry, both may express anger similarly, and both may become angry equally often, but the social and personal meanings attached to anger may be quite different for the sexes. At least to some extent, Tavris (1992) was correct when she said that "gender, like culture, organizes for its members different influence strategies, ways of communicating, nonverbal language and ways of perceiving the world" (291).

Table 3
Perceptions of Generalized Anger: Percentage
Answering "Always" or "Often"

	Female	Male	P
How often do you think members of your sex feel angry toward members of the opposite sex?	39.7	23.7	.000
How often do you think members of the opposite sex feel angry toward members of your sex?	39.4	30.1	.001

CORRELATES OF GENDER-BASED ANGER

Women and men do not exist in a vacuum; they are always situated in a specific context. Being part of a male or female subculture can, and often does make a difference in the way emotions are experienced and expressed, but other factors must also be examined. Structural theories of emotion assume that emotion is directly linked to one's social position (Smith-Lovin 1995).

Various researchers have explored the influence of background characteristics on anger. Earlier, the question was, "Are men and women different when it comes to aspects of anger?" Now the question is, "Does being a certain kind of man or woman make a difference?" Check and Malamuth (1985) studied both the degree and correlates of "anger hostility" among Canadian students. They found that the men's average score was slightly higher than the women's (8.79 versus 7.57). Analysis of independent variables showed that men with low self-esteem, traditional gender role attitudes, adversarial sexual attitudes toward women, a history of sexual abuse, and who believe in rape myths generally score higher in hostility toward women. Men who are single rather than married, lonely and depressed, and from a lower socioeconomic background also score higher on hostility. The authors indicate that less is known about correlates of female hostility toward men, but they find that some of the same variables apply. Thus, being single, holding adversarial sex beliefs, having low self-esteem, and being lonely and depressed all are associated with higher hostility scores for women. The authors assume that hostility toward women or men is the same trait as general hostility (as defined by Buss and Durkee 1957) except that it is directed at a specified sex.

Astrachan (1986) interviewed around 400 men from various backgrounds and found high levels of anger, fear, and envy as a result of changing patterns of gender roles. He describes three negative patterns of behavior among his respondents. The most obvious pattern is hostility—either "gross and physical or subtle and Machiavellian" (15). He claims that when "inferior" people rebel, men become angry because their power is challenged and also because men are exposed to the "reality of [their] own powerlessness" (18). Astrachan does not believe that these changes create hardships for men only; he says they involve pain and struggle for both sexes. He found that blue-collar men expressed the most overt hostility to changes in women's roles and the changes they require in men, but that middle- and upper-middle-class men also showed signs of resistance. He also indicated that the men he interviewed generally seem to have an easier time accepting changes, such as the shifting balance of power, in their personal lives than in their public lives.

Gary (1986) explored the impact of demographic and sociocultural factors on interpersonal conflict between black men and women. He found that demographic variables were not significant predictors of male-female conflict. He identified some "trends" and pointed out that males under age thirty tended to have more conflict than those who were older; married men experienced more conflict than formerly married and never-married men; those with higher levels of education experienced less conflict; and low-income black men reported less conflict than high-income black men. Research by Thomas (1993) corroborates one of Gary's trends; she found that women aged thirty-four and under are most likely to express anger. Those over age thirty-five were the least likely to do so. Thomas also documents differences between married and single women in regard to the "anger in" dimension, with married women scoring lower than single women. The anger, however, was not limited to gender-related issues.

Eisler and Skidmore (1987) developed a scale to measure masculine gender role stress (MGRS), which identified specific situations that are generally judged to be more stressful for males than females. They found that men are likely to feel stressed in situations that reflect physical inadequacy, require emotional expressiveness of tender emotions (love, fear, hurt), involve subordination to women, make them feel intellectually inferior, and involve performance failure at work or in sex. Men who scored high on MGRS were more likely to report increased anger. Kopper and Epperson (1991) found that sex role identity was significantly related to anger proneness, expression and suppression of anger, and control of anger expression. Those with a masculine identity were more prone to anger, more likely to express anger openly, and less likely to control the expression of anger. Feminine and undifferentiated individuals were least likely to express anger outwardly; feminine and androgynous types were most likely to control anger expression. Overall, androgyous individuals seemed to have the healthiest anger management style; they were less likely to perceive a situation as anger provoking, less likely to respond with anger, more likely to control the experience and expression of anger, and less likely to suppress anger.

In my unpublished works I examined the relationship between six demographic variables (sex, race, age, income, education, and relationship status) and gender-based anger. The anger questions focused on specific areas of work (inside and outside the home), sexual relations, dominance, and understanding, as well as on the general state of affairs between women and men. Each of the five specific areas was broken into parallel sets of questions for males and females. Each question tapped the degree of anger (measured by self-report) associated with a particular statement. I found that all but one of the background variables— relationship status—predicted feelings of anger on at least some of the issues. The best overall predictors were sex, race, age, and education. Income had some effect, and relationship status had none (see Table 4). Sex was the best and most consistent predictor of anger. Whether the anger items dealt with specific issues or general male-female relations, women were always angrier than men on all items focusing on male behavior. Sex was not predictive of anger feelings when it came to female behavior, where women and men shared a single standard.

Race predicted feelings of anger in a much less consistent way. First, there was a reverse pattern for specific and general issues, with blacks being less upset about specific issues but more upset about the general way that men and women treat each other today. Within the specific set of issues, there was no consistency in regard to whether the items referred to women or men, and there were statistically significant differences for only four out of ten specific anger statements. Whites expressed more anger than blacks over men having greater job opportunities, men and women telling each other what to do, and women not caring about men's sexual feelings. The set of specific issues presented to the respondents may not have tapped the problems that blacks are upset about. Yet blacks clearly judge general relations between women and men in a more negative light than do white individuals.

Age was a good predictor of anger feelings for the specific issues only. Within this set of statements, the pattern was consistent in that younger individuals were angrier than older individuals. Younger respondents were angrier about men having greater job opportunities and rewards, men not doing their share of the housework, men and women telling each other what to do, women not caring about men's sexual feelings, and men not trying to understand women.

Income was an important influence primarily when it came to general feelings of anger toward men and women. Those with lower levels of income clearly harbored stronger feelings of anger than those with higher income levels. Only one specific item—women telling men what to do—was statistically significant, and here the pattern reverses itself, with higher-income individuals being angrier than low-income individuals.

Education turned out to be a good predictor for specific and generalized anger, but the pattern was reversed for the two types of issues. The more highly educated were more angry about specific issues but less angry about the general state of affairs between women and men. Besides being angry about men having greater job opportunities, those with higher levels of education were most upset about men and women telling each other what to do and men and women not caring about each other's feelings.

The results of this study point to the importance of sex, race, age, education, and income in predicting gender-based anger. Those who are female or black and those with less income and education express the greatest anger over the way men and women treat each other generally. Age has no effect on feeling angry about the way men and women treat each other generally. The picture becomes more complicated when posing specific conflict situations. Five out of the six

Table 4:
Mean Scores for Gender Anger for Six Demographic Variables

"It makes me angry when..."

	Men have greater job opportunities and rewards than women	Women have greater job opportunities and rewards than men	Men don't do their share of housework	Women don't do their share of housework	Men tell women what to do	Women tell men what to do	Men don't care about women's sexual feelings	Women don't care about men's sexual feelings	Men don't try to understand women	Women don't try to understand men	The way men treat women today makes me angry	The way women treat men today makes me angry
SEX												
Female	2.51*	3.61	2.26*	2.74	2.10*	2.69	2.19*	2.60	2.20*	2.53	2.61*	2.85
Male	3.11*	3.62	2.94*	2.86	2.57*	2.64	1.52*	2.65	1.75*	2.66	2.85*	2.93
RACE												
Black	2.83*	3.59	2.44	2.74	2.40*	2.90*	2.35	2.76*	2.35	2.65	2.37*	2.67*
White	2.66*	3.62	2.52	2.78	2.21*	2.55*	2.28	2.55*	2.41	2.52	2.84*	2.97*
AGE												
18-29	2.61*	3.52	2.41*	2.77	2.17*	2.58*	2.26	2.52*	2.40*	2.50	2.63	2.84
30-45	2.56*	3.65	2.40*	2.84	2.09*	2.61*	2.26	2.55*	2.34*	2.55	2.73	2.93
46-64	2.81*	3.64	2.60*	2.80	2.38*	2.69*	2.40	2.69*	2.39*	2.62	2.70	2.85
65+	3.09*	3.62	2.72*	2.62	2.65*	2.85*	2.39	2.79*	2.59*	2.64	2.80	2.92
INCOME												
Below 15	2.71	3.55	2.38	2.70	2.34	2.81*	2.22	2.70	2.32	2.63	2.43*	2.69*
15-25	2.70	3.68	2.50	2.82	2.34	2.76*	2.31	2.60	2.45	2.51	2.61*	2.89*
25-50	2.63	3.64	2.57	2.86	2.17	2.51*	2.32	2.47	2.43	2.59	2.78*	2.91*
50+	2.84	3.54	2.65	2.78	2.21	2.50*	2.43	2.57	2.50	2.58	3.20*	3.24*
EDUCATION												
No high school	3.10*	3.54	2.59	2.63	2.52*	2.83*	2.49*	2.88*	2.48	2.64	2.30*	2.47*
High school	2.79*	3.54	2.54	2.73	2.36*	2.72*	2.36*	2.64*	2.41	2.60	2.62*	2.82*
Post high school	2.67*	3.66	2.46	2.81	2.22*	2.61*	2.26*	2.58*	2.38	2.53	2.74*	2.90*
College	2.50*	3.67	2.53	2.88	2.07*	2.56*	2.24*	2.48*	2.42	2.56	3.07*	3.23*
STATUS												
Married	2.77	3.63	2.57	2.79	2.27	2.67	2.37	2.62	2.42	2.60	2.77	2.93
Never married	2.54	3.51	2.36	2.69	2.15	2.64	2.19	2.56	2.36	2.48	2.63	2.82
Divorced	2.63	3.71	2.38	2.73	2.25	2.71	2.30	2.71	2.28	2.63	2.45	2.68
Separated	2.76	3.64	2.48	2.85	2.39	2.88	2.30	2.52	2.58	2.63	2.66	2.38
Widowed	2.88	3.55	2.57	2.83	2.49	2.67	2.32	2.71	2.52	2.56	2.73	2.90
Living together	2.50	3.76	2.53	3.10	2.19	2.24	2.19	2.52	2.38	2.62	2.86	2.90

Note: Asterisk(*) numbers indicate statistically significant differences at the .05 level (or less). Means can range from "1" (strongly agree) to "5" (strongly disagree).

background variables play a role in understanding an anger reaction to specific behaviors on the part of females and males, but the effect varies depending on the issue. Generally men's behavior elicits greater anger than women's behavior. For example, those who are female, white, young, and highly educated get angry about men's greater job opportunities and rewards. None of these background variables explain anger toward women who have greater job opportunities and rewards. This may be because people perceive this to be an unlikely scenario. The other situation that brings out angry reactions most consistently is the one dealing with dominance. Four of the five variables have predictive power in reference to men and women telling each other what to do.

Although the patterns are not simple, this research points out that reactions of anger vary in complex ways with the background of the individuals. Sex, race, or education may not help to predict anger reactions for one situation, but they may do so in another. The fact that predictions differed depending on whether the anger item was specific or general points out the importance of asking questions in different ways.

IMPLICATIONS

The societal changes discussed in a previous chapter and many of the research findings presented in this chapter lead one to believe that both women and men feel a fair amount of anger when it comes to how they see each other and the gender-related changes around them, but that probably women experience more anger. Kemper (1978, 1987), who developed a social relational theory based on social exchange principles, claims that relative positions on the dimensions of status and power influence emotional outcomes. Thus, for example, a loss of power produces feelings of depression or anxiety if the loss is perceived as irremediable, but anger if the loss is seen as remediable. In the context of male-female relationships, males are more likely to experience a loss of power and status, but it is not clear whether anger or depression is the result since it depends on the meanings assigned to this situation. According to Herbert Freudenberger (1987), today's men are troubled, and "one of the main problems they face is that of being male" (46). Men no longer are sure about their sexual relationships with women and their commitments to family and work. He identifies several sources of these problems: a greater emphasis on material achievement, changes in sexual stereotypes and norms, the rise of feminism, the lack of intimacy between men, and the unavailability of mentors. Men today do not know how to relate to women who are pursuing their own desires and needs. Male-female relationships increasingly have become concerned with power and control issues. Not knowing where they fit and how they should feel, many men turn to work and play, where they feel a greater sense of control and power. These confused, vulnerable, and uncomfortable men have no one to turn to. Older men too are anxious and troubled. Consequently, the only comfortable man-to-man relationships seem to be characterized by competition and rivalry. Men must reevaluate their priorities, says Freudenberger, and must get in touch with their feelings and learn to see others (women and men) as "loving collaborators in personal relationships" (47).

If there is any validity to his reasoning, it may be that men are more likely to be anxious and confused than angry and hostile. On the other hand, a social-psychological perspective asserts that anger is a more comfortable response than anxiety. The expression of anger reduces anxiety because anger externalizes problems and reduces feelings of insecurity. The experience of injustice reduces self-respect and diminishes status and self-control. Expressing anger at injustice makes one feel powerful and in control of a situation (Tedeschi and Nesler 1993).

Research on equity shows that people get angry when they give more than they get. This would probably predict greater anger on the part of females, who tend to be cast in the role of nurturer and giver more often than men. Those who work with the concepts of equity and distributive justice predict a relationship between expectations and emotions so that when people's expectations are not met, they become angry. This could predict anger on the part of women and men if they have expectations (similar or different) that are not being fulfilled.

Research conducted in the area of mental health generally finds greater levels of distress on the part of females, and to the extent that distress translates into anger, one would predict more anger for women than men. Another line of research shows men to be the less critical, less discerning ones in relationships and women more critical and more attuned to the problem areas. Again, this would lead to potentially greater anger on the part of females.

According to the "structural-strain" viewpoint (discussed by Mirowsky and Ross 1995) women's position in our society exposes them to greater hardship and constraint in both the home and workplace. Thus, women are in both structural and personal positions that motivate them to change what they have. Egalitarian ideology and greater structural resources combine to make women less satisfied and allow them to do something about it. The women's movement has been instrumental in crystallizing women's thoughts and feelings and giving concrete support for action and the vision for a different life.

I became sensitized to anger between the sexes as a result of my teaching. Some years ago, I noticed that the level of tension and uneasiness was rising when we covered the topic of gender roles. I started to teach in the mid-1970s and although there has always been a lot of interest in gender topics, there had been little tension and hostility. From the beginning, a certain proportion of women in these classes were indignant about the way men treat women and some resented the way some women let men trample all over them, but generally things were calm. A few years later, I noticed changes. The women in class now made more negative and hostile comments about men. The emphasis shifted from, "A woman who works outside the home shouldn't have to do all the housework," to "Men are lazy and I'm not sure I ever want to marry one!" Some of their most vitriolic comments came in response to men's sexual behavior. Throughout this time, the men in the class had been mostly silent when the women made derogatory comments. Some looked angry, some got red in the face, some smiled, some felt guilty, and some were remorseful, but most declined to comment. Then the men tried to justify male actions and privileges: "The reason we are so dedicated to our jobs and won't help with the housework is because we do all this for you."

Recently, more and more men have been willing to stand up for their own sex and openly, and sometimes angrily, challenge what the women say. Although they might admit to being "sexual boors," it was the women's fault! This, of course, incensed the women, and so back and forth it went. The atmosphere became charged as each defended themselves against the other's accusations. In some ways this situation has resulted in hypersensitivity to any negative remark about men, whether or not it is based on fact. Thus, talking about men raping women becomes "male bashing."

These classroom observations were mirrored in the society at large as public attention focused on the Hill–Thomas hearings, military scandals, and similar other situations, and I became increasingly curious about the state of anger between women and men. I've reported the results of the surveys I completed. Starting with chapter 5, I share the results of the interviews I completed in the spring of 1997. The interviews themselves were a joy; the frustrating part was that I had so many more questions than I could reasonably ask of people who all had busy lives. I was looking for answers to the following general questions:

1. What did these individuals learn about anger as they grew?
2. How did they deal with anger when they were young? How do they deal with it today? How comfortable are they with their own anger and with others' anger?
3. What makes them angry? Who makes them angry? Do they share their anger?
4. Does the other person's sex influence their anger expression mode?
5. Do they think women and men are different when it comes to anger?
6. What are their general thoughts on anger?
7. What makes them angry about men and women they know personally?
8. What makes them angry about men and women in general?
9. What angers them about how men and women treat each other?
10. How often do they get angry at men and women?
11. How angry are others at them?
12. What are their perceptions of how angry men are at women, women at men, and why are they angry at each other?
13. What are serious problems between women and men?
14. What could be done to improve relations between the sexes?
15. How do they feel about gender-related changes?
16. What is the ideal way to deal with anger?

A few other questions were asked as well, though not of all individuals.

Part II

Anger: Experience and Perception

Chapter 5

General and Anger Backgrounds of Participants

Signs of anger between women and men seem pervasive. One can hardly be a participant of informal female talk sessions without hearing about all the frustrations generated by men. It is equally difficult to read newspapers and magazines or listen to television shows without getting the message that relationships between men and women have developed some serious fault lines. However, I wondered to what extent media "war stories" reflect what is going on in ordinary people's lives. One of the men I interviewed for this book mentioned a talk show episode on television in which a husband viciously and angrily berated his wife for being overweight. This young man laughed and said that if he based his sense of what was going on between women and men in our society on what he saw on television, he'd think that the world was about to come to an end. Instead, he looks to friends and acquaintances when making judgments about the state of gender relations.

My earlier research projects left no doubt that a significant number of people (especially women) feel anger toward the other sex. These projects, however, were limited both by format (fixed-choice questions) and by content. More questions needed to be asked, and in an open-ended style. Both women and men had to be interviewed; otherwise, as Carole Tavris (1989) put it, "To listen to the grievances of one sex and not the other is to hear the sound of one hand clapping" (281).

The aim of this research was to gain a better and fuller understanding of the extent, sources, and perceptions of gender-based anger in ordinary women and men, as well as to explore their views on how to deal with anger and how to improve relationships between the sexes generally.

The word I put out was that I was writing a book on men, women, and anger and that I wanted to talk to ordinary (not necessarily angry) women and men about these issues. Several friends who had access to large numbers of people outside the university context helped to identify potential interviewees. In order to avoid miscommunication, a short description of the goals of the study was provided for individuals who had questions about the study. Along the way, quite a few people offered to contact a particularly angry person they knew. I declined these offers. Apparently, the process worked fairly well because a lot of people would preface the interview with, "I don't know how useful I will be because I'm not really an angry person." The interviews took place in the context of Greenville, North Carolina a small, southern city, and surrounding counties. The findings from these interviews cannot be generalized to other settings, but they provide a sense of how individuals in a semirural, southern setting view various gender-related issues and anger in their own and others' lives. The fact that these interviews took place in the South must raise the possibility that respondents, particularly women who were born and raised there, might be reticent to share their feelings about anger since a premium is put on being polite, restrained, and friendly. One woman who was raised to be a "southern lady" recalls being told specifically that "girls do not get angry." To this day she admits to being confused about anger and wonders whether her periods of depression are really masked anger.

The interview questions were structured around three areas of inquiry. The first set of questions focused on the family and the anger background of these individuals—their past and present experiences with anger in general. Our anger repertoire and the way we relate to men and women in our lives is at least partly conditioned by what we encountered in our family of origin and our early experiences with anger. The questions focusing on anger in general were followed by a series of questions that explored anger in the context of gender. Respondents were asked about the role of gender on anger expression and the extent and the sources of their own anger toward men and women, as well as their perceptions of what made others (women and men) angry. The third section of the interview contained questions that tapped respondents' feelings about recent gender-related changes, problems between women and men, and ways to improve relationships between the sexes. Later in the interview process I added a few additional questions dealing with feelings about being a man or a woman and the future of the sexes. The interview concluded with a series of short background questions on age, race, education, occupation, relationship status, number of children, religiosity, sex of friends, and attitudes toward women's rights. The typical interview lasted around one hour, with some extending to two to three hours.

GENERAL BACKGROUND CHARACTERISTICS OF STUDY PARTICIPANTS

The men and women who agreed to be interviewed varied widely in terms of background characteristics. The women ranged in age from twenty-four to sixty, though most were in their thirties and forties. The average age was forty (overall, they shared 1,006 years worth of wisdom). The youngest male was twenty-one, and the oldest male was seventy-five. More males were in their forties and fifties than twenties or thirties; the average age was forty-six (1,158 years worth of wisdom). Most of the participants were white, with the rest black. Almost all of the participants, male and female, were employed most with full-time jobs; only four women were unemployed, and three males were unemployed (due to retirement). Most participants worked in a white-collar setting (at various levels), but several blue-collar occupations (beautician, bus driver, security guard, food server) were represented.

The women and men were in various relationship states, with the majority of males and females married (65 percent of the females and 72 percent of the males) at the time of the interview. Although only three women and two men were divorced at the time of the interviews, many more (ten) had been previously divorced and were now in second and third marriages. Four men and three women were currently single; one woman was widowed, one was separated, and one was engaged. One-fifth of the group had no children, and everyone else had at least one child, with most having two or three; almost all were biological children. Two of the women and one man had children from previous nonmarital relationships.

Overall, this group had high levels of education. Only one person had less than a high school education; three had stopped with high school (one was a general equivalency diploma). About half of the overall group had a college degree, and many had taken some college courses at either a community college or a four-year institution. Almost half of the group identified themselves as very religious (more females than males) though some of these rejected the term *religious* since it is associated with procedure rather than content. These individuals preferred to call themselves "Christians" or said that God was very important in their lives. Not all of those who professed a strong belief in God attended church either regularly or at all. Close to another third of the individuals identified themselves as "fairly" or "moderately" religious, and the rest had their own brand of spirituality or were agnostic, atheist, or "confused."

Participants were asked about the sex of their close friends. Men (more than half) were much more likely to say their close friends are evenly divided among males and females, while only a third of the females described this situation. When friends were unevenly mixed, males and females were equally likely to say that more of their friends were of the same sex. The other situation, having mixed friends but more of them of the other sex, was relatively rare. None of males interviewed said that their close friends were either all male or all female, and several of the females had only female friends while one said her closest friends were all males. Clearly, the preferred pattern for both the women and men in this sample was to have friendships with members of both sexes. However, females were much more likely to rely on single-sex friends (especially of the female sex) than were males. A couple of men specifically mentioned that they stayed away from having only female friends in order to avoid potential hard feelings on the part of their wives.

There was little variation in the participants' support of equal rights, opportunities, and obligations for women and men. The overwhelming majority of females and males shared a belief in gender equality. In fact, more males supported it than females. One female simply believed that women and men should not have the same rights and obligations; she liked the traditional setup. Six females and two males (almost all devout Christians) believed in equal rights and opportunities but not in equal obligations. They felt strongly that men and women have somewhat different God-ordained obligations, which demand that the male take a leadership role, at least in the home.

FAMILY BACKGROUND OF FEMALE PARTICIPANTS

To begin the interview I asked each individual to tell me about the family he or she grew up in. Although this question was designed primarily to get the participant comfortable, it led to interesting and unexpected findings. Of the twenty-five women, more than half (fifteen) came from families that had suffered one or more serious stressful conditions, ranging from prolonged, bitter fighting to physical and sexual abuse. Only seven women described their family backgrounds as close and loving and mentioned no particular negative experience. One other woman talked about her family of origin in positive terms but mentioned that her father's harsh criticism and anger made life difficult. It struck me repeatedly that the various traumatic experiences these individuals described seemed at odds with the image they presented. It seemed incredible that these perfectly calm, well-mannered, kind, intelligent, socially poised women could have gone through such hard and sometimes horrific experiences. As sociologists are fond of saying, surfaces are deceitful. After talking to so many women who had gone through such painful experiences and yet were making or had made a success of their own lives and families, my faith in human willpower and human resourcefulness was replenished.

Close to one-third (seven) of the women had experienced divorce when they were young (one woman experienced divorce three times between age five and adulthood). Typically, the divorce occurred when they were young (below age ten). One woman talked about growing up in an "arguing and fighting family" where the father, who "did not know how to communicate," was harsh toward the wife and children. Her way to deal with it was to leave as soon as she could (at age sixteen) and, as she said, she "has been taking care of [herself] ever since." The parents later divorced, but she feels that she did not have much of a childhood, had bad role models, and reflects, "It took me thirty-seven years to realize why I was the way I was." In this case, it might have been better if the divorce had occurred when she was young.

As a result of divorce, various living arrangements had been experienced while growing up. One woman and her sister lived with her father after the divorce and visited her mother and her new husband twice a week. Several ended up living with grandparents as the result of divorce or because the parents were unable to care for their child. A couple of women ended up with stepfathers who were generally seen as cold, critical, and domineering.

The most striking finding to come from the material on family background is the powerful, destructive impact that many of the fathers had. Out of the group of women who had come from unhappy and conflicted backgrounds, it was almost always the father (either biological or stepfathers) who had wreaked the greatest emotional and physical havoc in the respondents' childhood.

The most negative memories involved fathers with a military background. One middle-aged woman remembers that when her father came home to retire, "the whole atmosphere in the house shifted." Where in his absence there had been a lot of open expression, now there was a lot of fear, and family members shut their mouths. She describes her father as a mean, manipulative, and extremely controlling person, who sexually abused her and her three sisters to varying degrees. Her mother had no idea of this situation and was not told until many years later. This woman carried anger around for a long time and says that everything she did was reactionary. It was not until many years later that she was able to rid herself of the anger associated with those early years. She was, and still is, incredulous about how such abuse can happen without anybody else knowing about it. Another woman's father, also a military man, was described as a strong disciplinarian, an emotional and physical abuser, an alcoholic, and a mean man with an explosive temper. As one of eight children, she never received any word of encouragement, and she and her siblings were frequently beaten for as little as singing in the car while on a trip. This woman recited a horrifying list of cruel and vicious acts that her father perpetrated on the children, the mother, and hired help. She saw her mother as wonderful but very controlled and very afraid of her husband. The good times "were far and few between." Her mother died early, and she considers this a blessing because it allowed the mother to escape this destructive situation. Today, this woman is struggling mightily with the aftermath of childhood trauma and has made tremendous progress in dealing with the anger and hurt in her life. Most of her siblings have been married several times and continue to have relationship problems, which she attributes to a large extent to the emotional legacy of their father.

Several other women related stories about fathers who were harsh, uncommunicative, critical, and emotionally distant and controlling or fathers who would not support their wife and children, fathers who drank too much, and fathers who had affairs openly. Although mothers were not always portrayed as loving and wonderful—some were seen as too strict or as too weak, as too dependent (in relation to their husbands) or as too uninvolved—none evoked the level of fear, hatred, and pain that so many of the fathers did.

On the positive side, around one-fourth of the women reported close and loving parental relationships. In one case, the father was clearly the preferred parent and was described as her idol. In several other cases, there were no strong negative or positive feelings expressed about the nature of the child-parent bond or the relative influence of mother versus father. Only one father was identified as being actively involved in child rearing.

The majority of the women (seventeen) came from a southern background though not necessarily North Carolina. The respondents were mixed fairly evenly in regard to urban versus rural background. Most had grown up in a lower- to middle-class lifestyle. Several mentioned that they had been poor according to today's standards but that they don't remember feeling deprived or lacking for anything important.

FAMILY BACKGROUND OF MALE PARTICIPANTS

The men's backgrounds varied widely. A number of them came from families with three or more children; in fact, three of the men came from poor and very large families, with eight or more siblings. Roughly half of the men had a middle- to upper-class background, and the other half had come from a lower-class background. Most had been reared in some region of the South. The majority came from an intact family background, with one-fifth having experienced a divorce and one the death of his father.

The emotional milieus ran the gamut from very happy and close relations to bitter, angry, and distant relations between family members. One-fifth of the male respondents described a basically happy, untroubled family of origin. Slightly less than that also remembered close and warm family situations but marred by problems, typically revolving around the fathers' behaviors and attitudes. Slightly more than one-fifth of the respondents spoke of harsh, tense, unhappy childhoods, and in all but one of these the father was seen as the major source of conflict and pain. In one case, the mother was remembered in an extremely negative light, and in two other cases, the mother was mentioned along with the father as having wreaked emotional or physical havoc. Thus, the men's descriptions of their families of origin echoed the women's to a large extent.

Again, the stories provided evidence of a powerful, negative influence of fathers. Even of those families described as having basically been happy, loving, and supportive, half of them had problems caused by the father. (This was unsolicited information; the respondents simply were asked to talk about the family they came from.) Slightly less than a third of the families of origin were depicted as not particularly loving or close. Most of these had no particular problems or traumas, but of the few that did, again, it was perceived to be the father's fault.

The types of behaviors the fathers exhibited ranged from being "tense and yelling a lot" to extreme anger, sarcasm, and physical abuse. The mildest problem was having a father who expected his son to be as perfect as himself, thus putting great pressure on a child who felt he could not live up to these expectations. This individual did feel that his dad was easing up a bit as he grew older. One middle-aged man described his father as having a "rough streak" and as having been a competitive, impatient, angry, and very bitter man. Some of these traits were instilled in his son, who today is trying very hard to reduce his anger and impatience. Growing up in a family with eleven other siblings, one man recalls feelings of closeness and having lots of fun but characterizes his father as a self-centered, self-focused, and demanding man. This same man says his mother was gentle, docile, and undemanding (to a fault). One man spoke of tension in the house because of his father's unpredictable temper.

Other male respondents shared particularly poignant and bitter memories of their fathers. One grew up in an upper-middle-class home with a successful but alcoholic, extremely rigid, hot-tempered, angry father (and a perfectionist mother). There was a lot of anger and fighting in his home, but he thinks that in this type of home, you become numb to it and begin to accept it as normal. He believes that his sister intentionally got pregnant in high school in order to get out of the house. The man she married was unacceptable to her father, and he literally put all of her things in the yard and told the son that from now on, his sister was "dead." After she left, it was up to him to fulfill all parental expectations, an impossible task, which left him wondering, "Does anybody love me?" Another man, who classifies his family as "dysfunctional," speaks of a childhood that was marred by moving a lot (due to his father's job) and by his father's inability to be a good father; "We all sort of suffered from my father who was not a very good father" is how he put it. He said that at one point, everyone except his dad was in therapy, talking about problems with his dad. His younger brother was diagnosed as manic-depressive, and a lot of his problems were attributed to the negative relationship with his father. After twenty-seven years of marriage, his father left his mother, "without warning." Upon his father's leaving, this man got extremely angry, and "a lot of stuff from earlier years came pouring out." Another man recalls his father as an angry man and how he "woke up every morning to his father's screaming and had dinner every night with his father screaming at the table."

In three cases, the mother was also mentioned in a negative light. One was a perfectionist who contributed to the tension and anxiety in her son's life by putting tremendous pressure on him to fulfill impossible expectations. The other mother was described as "not very loving" and having an "I don't care" attitude. Although there were eight children in this home and the father worked full-time, he remembers days when no dinner would be cooked. A third man recalls a traumatic childhood with a bitter, angry mother who was an alcoholic and became very physical when she got drunk. For the rest of the men, either the mother was not singled out for discussion in any particular way or she was mentioned with affection, respect, and empathy.

The disturbing role that fathers seem to play in these men's lives was not an expected finding. It seemed incredible that in almost half of the cases, the father was brought up as having caused a lot of tension, pain, and suffering. For many of these men (and the women), such early exposure to tension, fear, and anger became a motivator for avoiding certain behaviors and attitudes. In that sense, some good came of the pain. Several people specifically mentioned that they swore to do things differently because of what they had gone through with their fathers.

ANGER IN THE FAMILY OF ORIGIN

The family is the place where all of us should learn to navigate the treacherous currents generated by powerful emotions such as anger. The same can be said for sexuality. Just as all of us will encounter anger in our lives, we will participate in sexual relationships, and basic guidelines and values should be provided by our family of origin. Studies indicate that the great majority of parents do not provide any meaningful sex education for their children. I wondered whether parents had acted more responsibly when it came to anger. Therefore, I asked respondents several questions whose aim it was to find out what they had been taught and what they had experienced in regard to anger.

Anger Background of Female Participants

Only nine of the twenty-five women said that anger was discussed in the family while they were growing up, and what they were told was not always helpful. One woman said she remembers her mom telling her, "If somebody hits you, hit them back!" Besides being told to stick up for herself, she was told that it was wrong to fight where others can see you. Apparently her parents practiced what they preached because they never fought in front of the two children; when they announced their divorce, the daughters were in shock, since they thought all was going well in their parents' lives. While growing up, she observed her father's habit of going into the garage whenever he was angry. When she asked him about it, he said: "I figure I'll go out to the garage and I'll cool off, and when I come back in, if I'm calmed down, it's not worth yelling about." Although she greatly admired her father for this attitude, she did not adopt this technique herself.

A second woman was simply told to "let it go!" Nevertheless, she watched her mother hold her anger in all the time and took after her. Another was expected to "stuff it!" She was not allowed to voice any criticism or negative feelings to her mother or stepfather. Her stepfather, in particular, would not allow any expression of anger or any challenge to his authority. If during dinner she would mention that she didn't like the vegetable then he would put more on her plate. She vividly remembers choking on some food that she was trying to get down and he said, "If you throw that up I'll make you eat it." This woman learned to hold her feelings in at least as a child. Interestingly enough, her parents often had loud, explosive fights and arguments. A woman who had been raised in a traditional southern home learned from an early age that it was inappropriate for girls to show anger, and she took this lesson to heart. Years later, she is somewhat confused about recognizing anger in herself and is working on ways to express anger in a constructive manner.

"If you can't say something nice don't say anything at all" is what another woman was told by her mother. Another woman remembers being told that it was important to control anger, to talk about the conflict after calming down. This message is very much in line with what therapists are advising today. Good advice was also given to a woman who learned "never go to bed angry" and "let the other person know how you feel." A young black woman remembers learning that it was absolutely wrong ever to show anger toward an authority figure in any way "You could not even squint your eyes!" she laughed. Finally, another woman learned that she had to get herself under control before Daddy got home because "when daddies get home, they are tired and don't want to deal with upset, crying little girls."

Although the majority of the other respondents didn't remember any specific discussions or teachings about anger, many of them assimilated various lessons from observation and experience and in reaction to a particular parent's style. At around age six, one woman remembers being terribly upset because her parents were arguing and fussing at the dinner table and she assumed that this meant they were going to divorce. Upon discovering her fear, her parents explained that arguing and disagreeing are normal in a marriage, an explanation that has been helpful in her own marriage today. Another woman grew up in a home where emotion of any kind was rarely shown except for yelling and screaming between her brothers and her father and some yelling on the part of her mother. She recalls hating it when people got angry or there was any kind of conflict. She adopted her mother's style, which was to swallow anger for a long time and then to explode. She said that she tried to avoid conflict for most of her adult life, but after a recent clinical depression, she has become much more assertive and is not afraid of conflict anymore.

Several women grew up in homes where parents either rarely or never fought in front of the children, thus teaching them that public display of anger is wrong. A couple of women were surrounded by parents or siblings who fought frequently and openly. These women, to their later regret, adopted a similar style for themselves, learning that anger is not to be held in and to speak their negative thoughts freely.

One woman said that somewhere along the way she developed the idea that anger is a negative emotion that requires some control. Although she no longer sees anger as totally negative, she does continue to believe that it needs to be controlled. Several women mentioned that they learned incorrect and sometimes contradictory ways from watching their parents. Typically, one parent (almost always the father) had an explosive temper, and often the other parent tended to be quiet. The daughters hated the way their father acted or were afraid of him and usually modeled themselves after their mothers and learned to clam up and keep the anger in, thus substituting one extreme reaction for another. One middle-aged black woman recalls that her father, a generally angry man who took offenses personally, would explode physically and verbally. She was terrified of him as a child and wouldn't ask him anything; if her mother said, "Go ask your father," in response to a request, she would forgo whatever she wanted rather than have to talk to him. In response to his aggressive and explosive behavior and her mother's cool composure, she learned to hold feelings in. She decided that she would not act on "raw emotion" as her father had. With her own children today, she does things very differently; she does not use physical punishment and tries to stay calm and rational. She laughs and says, "it's a trade-off; they [the children] don't listen as well, but they are not scared of me!"

In other cases, the parents' negative behaviors acted as strong motivators for adopting constructive patterns. One mother's way of dealing with anger had a tremendous impact on her daughter; whenever the mother got angry, she would refuse to talk to family members and this could last for weeks. The daughter hated this silence with a passion and would have preferred almost anything else besides being totally shut out. As a result of this experience, she vowed that she would never do this to her children; there would never be anything that would make her so mad that she wouldn't talk to them about it. So far, she has kept her promise to herself.

Another woman lived with parents who fought routinely and saw how the fights escalated because one or the other kept pushing until the whole situation got blown way out of proportion. She says this taught her two things; first, when you provoke somebody, you better be ready to accept what's coming, and second, you need to be able to walk away from a fight before it gets out of hand. Although she used to start arguments and "egg things on," increasingly she has learned how to walk away from a potentially explosive situation.

One respondent lived in a home where children "should be seen but not heard" and observed two parents with very different styles. Her father would get upset over every little thing, and her mother would stay totally calm no matter what. The lesson she took away was that one should not get angry over stupid, little stuff but that it's okay to get angry over some things, thus forging for herself a combination of the two parents' styles.

Anger Background of Male Participants

Each man was also asked what he had been taught about anger while growing up. Only four of the twenty-five remembered being talked to about anger. One man was told not to let the night go down on his wrath or to deal with emotions immediately and not to carry a big chip. His dad also taught him "to get others now before they get you" and that it's a dog-eat-dog world and that he needs to be in control. From listening to his father's words and by watching him (his father had an explosive temper) he said he learned how to be angry, driven, and impatient; he was a quick-tempered child who had to win at everything. He was extremely submissive to his father and to other authority figures in general.

A second man recalls being admonished by his mother not to get angry and not to fight and never to get angry in public. He was given no specific advice on what to do if he did get angry or how to avoid getting into fights. This man never saw his parents argue as a child. One day when he and his brother returned from boy scout camp, their parents sat them down and told them they were getting divorced. Although his father and mother never argued in front of the children, he had seen his father yell and scream when angry, although when someone else was angry his father would simply withdraw. Whenever an anger episode involved his troubled older brother, his father would always withdraw and let the mother handle it.

The third man who remembers direct conversation about anger was told by his mother, "If you don't have anything nice to say, don't say anything at all." He never remembers his mom saying anything bad about anybody until he was grown. In retrospect, he thought her advice and behavior were harmful because he learned to keep his mouth shut and hold his feelings in. The fourth man learned that it's all right to express anger, not to take things into his own hands, and to take time to cool off. Besides being told these things, he, his sister, and his mother had family devotions and discussions about feelings, which have helped him to deal with anger more than anything else. His mother would ask them to write down what bothered them most about what the other was doing, and they then shared their thoughts and talked about solutions. Sometimes they made up code words so that each could let the other know when he or she was doing something troublesome without others around them knowing.

The rest of the men could not remember any specific learnings or conversations dealing with any aspect of anger. Through observation and experience, they adopted various positions. Several learned that it's all right to be angry and express anger because they saw their parents (usually the father) do it. One man, now in his early forties, grew up with a father who exploded a lot. During a typical dinner, his dad would explode over any number of things, such as his wife's forgetting to heat up his plate. His father would not only yell, curse, and complain but hit the table with his fist and sometimes walk out on them. As a child, he mimicked his father's behavior by getting irrational when angry, getting into physical fights, and yelling and cussing; he also would "stew over" things and hold grudges for a long time. As an adult, he no longer is physically aggressive and typically not verbally aggressive. He says he is much more able "to hold his own counsel now" and to think things through before reacting.

Others became determined *not* to copy their parents' violent, explosive, and sometimes unpredictable temperament. One young man talked about how his father had a big temper and would react in extreme ways, even in public. Having suffered through many embarrassing situations, he knew he did not want to lose his temper the way his father had. A middle-aged professional had a "loud, screaming daddy" and a controlling mother, and he became cautious when it came to emotions because he learned that anger could get you in a lot of trouble and that "it would pretty much tear people around you up." It was the combination of his mother's and father's actions and demeanors that taught another man and his siblings to be close-mouthed and not to get involved in highly emotional, angry encounters. His mother was an alcoholic who would get very physical and violent when she was drunk, and his sarcastic and condescending father knew how "to cut somebody down to nothing" with words. To this day, he says, he simply leaves and refuses to get involved when they start to fight with each other or when others are angry. His own anger style was physically aggressive (he "stomped" and beat on people and on doors) while growing up, although today he is much less physical and deals with the situation verbally and quickly and then lets it go "if he's allowed to."

Several men—mostly those who had parents who were rather reserved and rational about anger situations—mentioned that they had "somehow" absorbed the idea that it was wrong, was a sign of weakness, or was unmanly to show too much anger. This did not mean, however, that they stayed away from fights and anger, especially as children.

Relatively few studies look at familial socialization influences in regard to the emotions. Research reviewed by Brody and Hall (1993) shows that in general, parents tend to discuss emotions more with their daughters than their sons; however, this pattern does not hold with anger and other outer-directed emotions. Contrary to this, women in my sample were more likely to have been talked to about anger than the men (though the majority of them, women or men, were not talked to about anger). Research cited by Brody and Hall found that fathers and mothers used a different interaction style with their children, with fathers being more demanding, more threatening, more foul-mouthed, and more demeaning than mothers. This finding was corroborated by the results of my interviews.

From listening to the responses, it is clear that there is a strong connection between what happened as they were growing up and what they are today. This makes it imperative that parents model a positive, constructive style of anger management.

Women's Typical Childhood Anger Episodes

Each respondent was asked what typically happened when someone in her or his family was angry when she or he was growing up. When comparing the answers the females gave in reference to their mothers' and fathers' behaviors regarding anger expression, the pattern was striking: only four mothers typically yelled and screamed and expressed any physical aggression, while thirteen fathers yelled and screamed and sometimes became physically violent. Several women said that their parents did not show anger in front of them or that it was a rare event, so there was no typical situation to describe. A couple of women described their typical family episode as a fairly calm event. The majority remembered loud, explosive, and sometimes violent anger episodes while growing up. The participants in these varied considerably. Usually the father was the one who would vent his anger in the loudest and most explosive way. A few mothers yelled and screamed, and in all of these cases, their spouse was also loud and explosive. The typical pattern was for the father to be the explosive one and the mother to be the calm one. Sometimes the mothers would fuss or nag, or cry, or say, "Oh, spit!" but generally mothers maintained a composed exterior. One woman remembers her mother explaining to her that men don't know what to do with emotions.

Some episodes involved all family members, though not necessarily all at the same time. For example, in one family, everyone said exactly what they thought, and this created lots of turmoil—yelling, screaming, cursing, throwing, hitting—

but none of it was aimed at the father, whom everyone was terrified of. This particular father was a mean, violent, and hot-tempered man who yelled and screamed and hit everyone else at one time or another. Fights in one home got so bad that an older sibling was asked to leave home. The respondent described her father as a man with a very hot temper who would leave the house in a fury when angry. The mother dealt with her anger by claming up and crying.

In a couple of cases, the explosions were between the siblings; the parents were calm. One typical anger situation occurred primarily between the woman's brothers and their father. The final pattern that was reported by the women was a mixture of experiences that did not usually involve explosive anger on anyone's part. In one family, the father always washed dishes and cleaned things and refused to talk when he was mad. This behavior angered her mother, who wanted to talk about the issues. Another woman remembers a lot of crying when someone was angry. She said that her mom cried a lot because of her stepfather, a critical, negative person. Whenever her mom was angry, she would give "bad looks." In another home, a lot of doors were slammed and people left, but there was not too much arguing back and forth because people held feelings in. One brother held things in until he exploded, but another brother was described as hardly ever getting angry—as being "like a dishrag," with no visible emotions. This brother also molested her sexually as she was growing up. Another woman recounted her grandfather's sitting her down and calmly talking to her about the situation. He never raised his voice. Her grandmother tended to nag when angered.

Men's Typical Childhood Anger Episodes

The pattern for the male respondents was identical to that of the female respondents: fathers were more likely to be loud and explosive than mothers, only not as pronounced. Overall, the majority of these men grew up in homes where at least one parent (sometimes both) expressed anger in a loud and explosive way. It was interesting to note that no loud and explosive mother was paired with a calm, quiet, and reserved man (in one situation the father was a lot calmer than the mother, but he tended to be quite destructive without raising his voice), while the reverse pattern was quite common. In a handful of cases, respondents said that anger was handled in a calm and quiet way without shouting, door slamming, or cursing. Several men could not remember any typical anger episodes.

These people's experiences generally support deeply held anger and gender stereotypes of outwardly expressive men and emotionally reserved women. The stories also show that there is a lot of variety in the way anger was dealt with.

MODES OF ANGER EXPRESSION OVER TIME

Female Respondents, Then and Now

All were asked what they used to do when they were angry while they were growing up and what they do today. About half of the women said they typically held their anger feelings in when they were young. A couple of these adopted a combination of holding in and then exploding, but they were the exception. As a small child, one woman would not only hold her feelings in when mad but also held her breath until she passed out. Most retreated, either going to their room or taking a walk; they worked through their feelings by themselves. Many of the women who said they swallowed their anger also mentioned that they cried when angry, especially when they were "really angry." Interestingly enough, almost none of the women who tended to express their anger in some open manner mentioned crying as something they did when angry. It's almost as though the body must find some way of venting. Around one-fourth of the women said that they used to yell and scream and sometimes hit others when angry. A couple also expressed their feelings of anger but not in an explosive fashion. Two women said they could not remember what they did when angry.

What do these women do today when they're angry? Most of them are no longer doing what they used to do or are trying not to. Of those who tended to hold their anger inside, the overwhelming majority are, or are trying to be, more open and expressive with their feelings. These women realized along the way that their anger style was destructive in some fashion, and many have struggled to be able to express their frustrations and concerns in a positive way. One woman was raised in home where emotions of any kind were not shown. She remembers hating it when people got angry or there was any kind of conflict. She used to have her mother's style, which was to swallow anger for a long time and then explode. She said she tried to avoid conflict most of her adult life, but after a recent clinical depression, she has become much more aggressive and assertive and is no longer afraid of conflict or of saying what she feels. She works on sharing her feelings in ways that don't hurt or alienate others.

Several women had lived in a family where they were commonly exposed to angry encounters; they learned to hate confrontation and figured that the best thing they could do with their own anger and frustration was to keep it inside. Often they modeled themselves after their mothers, who tended to hide their negative emotions. In one case, the father had a hot temper, and the mother dealt with anger by "claming up and crying." This woman modeled herself after her mom and now, years later, has started trying to talk about her anger more and to get it out and be honest about her feelings as much as possible. She said that she now realizes that she doesn't "have to suffer with it." When she and her husband disagree, she will tell him what is bothering her instead of "seething inside and expecting him to try to figure out what is wrong."

One young woman, who had been unable to share her feelings throughout childhood and young adulthood, said she developed serious panic attacks around age nineteen and since then has been trying to be more open. She still cannot talk about her concerns and frustrations to her husband, who "totally intimidates" her or to her father, who used to "terrify" her. But she is trying to share some of her needs with others.

Another woman, following her father's footsteps, used to keep her anger and frustration inside, where it would seethe and grow; at some point she would lose her control and rant and rave. Today she no longer fumes in her mind but thinks about what she needs and how to get it and then takes steps to achieve those goals. She credits the book *When Anger Hurts* for helping her to become much more "proactive" in her approach to dealing with hurt feelings.

Overall, the majority of the female respondents now share their anger feelings at least to some extent or under certain circumstances. Some share their feelings only when they think it will do some good; others let only those close to them know they're angry (the most common pattern); others share negative feelings more easily with strangers; still others talk only about the important things and bite their tongue over little things, which they try to let go.

A few continue to do the same things, and they seem unhappy about the lack of change. One woman in her forties, who used to suppress her anger (especially at her stepfather), says that today, "Unfortunately, I do the same damn thing!" She believes that because she is not a very confrontational person, she keeps too much inside, and it takes "a lot of crap" before she gets angry; eventually she explodes. This woman knows that she needs to find a way to be able to tell people why she's angry so that a solution can be worked on, but she finds it very difficult to share feelings until she is at the point of explosion.

Of those who used to vent their anger freely, the majority have been working on gaining greater control over their anger and are succeeding to various degrees. One who used to "look for something to be angry about" and could get angry over "anything" and let all her anger and criticism out freely, recently began to struggle with the anger in her life with the help of a therapist. She now works on sharing her anger in nondestructive, assertive ways and for the first time sees hope and says, "You can't imagine how it feels not to be a time bomb!" This woman had grown up in a highly stressful home where she was expected to be perfect by a father who terrorized the household. She is a survivor and provides testimony to the ability to change even relatively late in life.

A woman who had been angry frequently and vehemently says that it takes a lot to get her angry today and now expresses anger in a much milder manner. She also came out of a conflict-ridden home, and although she still bears scars and feels anger toward her family, especially her father, she believes that one "has to move on."

A woman who used to scream and lose control tries not to let her emotions rule her today. She believes in the importance of sharing what makes her angry but now does so assertively and calmly. She stresses the crucial role that prayer plays in her life and her ability to deal with and forgive anger in both herself and others.

One woman who was extremely open with anger feelings in the past continues to do so today but says she is not very comfortable with her anger. "I don't like it I think I yell too much I sometimes scare myself with it," she says about her anger today.

Two women who could not remember what they used to do are similar to each other in that both tend to work the anger out pretty much by themselves. One woman says she is very quiet when angry and works it out herself. She stressed that she and her spouse are calm people and that she doesn't get angry much; she has been angry enough to yell at him only two or three times in forty-some years of marriage. The second woman controls and decreases anger feelings by exercising and praying for those who anger her.

Thus, overall, the majority do share their anger feelings with others today, though most of those who let others know they're angry do so on a conditional basis. Clearly, the closer the relationship is, the more that people feel they can share anger. One woman is an exception, for she will not say anything to her husband (whom she is totally intimidated by) and to her father (who used to terrify her). She generally shares any anger only with those below her in social status.

Each woman was asked how comfortable she is today with her own anger, and the majority said they were comfortable to one degree to another. Only a handful expressed serious discomfort with their style of anger management. Several indicated that their level of comfort was the result of persistent struggle and help from others. One woman said she has learned to put things in perspective from a nurse manager and a cousin. The nurse manager told her that some things are not worth beating your head against a brick wall over, and thus she has learned that if she's mad over something she can't change but has to live with, she gets over it. It has taken her a long time to let things go, but words from a cousin also helped. This cousin once said that she wasn't going to let anybody "live rent free in her head." The respondent said that she learned from this that if she's angry at someone and doesn't talk to the person about that anger, it hurts her, not the other person. Though she is comfortable with her own anger today, she stresses that it took "a lot of prayer and working through things" in order to let the anger go.

A couple of the women have achieved a sense of control and comfort after help from a therapist. One of these women who used to be afraid of conflict and used to have trouble sharing her anger experienced a clinical depression, and after working things through with a therapist is comfortable with her own anger today. The other woman realized that she was ruining her husband and ultimately her marriage by her perfectionist and critical attitude and called a therapist.

Being comfortable with one's own anger does not mean that one is comfortable with others' anger, or vice versa. Even though most women are comfortable (to one degree or another) with their own anger, slightly more than half are not comfortable with others' anger, though several of these are working on becoming more comfortable. Some women are uncomfortable because they are afraid. For example, one woman says others' anger makes her nervous "a lot"; she has a fiancé who is sometimes cruel and comes close to hitting her, and she is afraid of his anger. Others have a tendency to feel guilty when someone is angry at them; they take things too personally and feel as if they have failed in some way. When feeling guilty, one woman says she overcompensates (just as her mother did). One woman says she is learning that she is not responsible for others' actions and tells herself that she does not have to receive others' anger.

Few are comfortable with others' anger without reservation. For many, their level of comfort depends on the situation or person. For example, one woman said she is comfortable dealing with her sons' anger but not with anybody else's because she remembers her husband's rage and father's verbal abuse. For another woman, it depends on whether the other's anger is justified. If it is, she'll deal with it; otherwise, she'll run away. One young woman laughed and said that she is intrigued when others are angry at each other and wants to find out what's going on. However, if the anger is aimed at her, she gets very nervous.

Male Respondents, Then and Now

About equal numbers of men tended to hide their anger when they were young and hold it inside or express it, usually in a fairly explosive manner. A few men could not remember what they used to do. One said he didn't get angry; he just sat and listened. He lived in a home where he says, "There was only one person who was allowed to be angry in my family, and that was my father." Like the women, most of the men have worked toward changing their style over time; the majority of those who held anger in have adopted a more open style today. Out of those who had yelled and screamed and sometimes hit, all but one have become calmer and more rational much of the time.

Very few experienced no changes, and most of these have been individuals who continue their childhood pattern of keeping anger to themselves. One young black man says it's hard to open up and say what is bothering him after keeping feelings inside for so long. He used to resolve anger with a bottle; if he was angry or upset, he would drink and then go to sleep and apologize in the morning. The only time he can share his feelings at all is when "it hurts real bad." And even then, he confides, he may not be able to do it directly but resorts to indirect ways, such as using another person to ask about something that he is really concerned about.

Today the majority share their anger feelings to some extent. A few never seem to have any problems letting others know when they're angry. One example is a man, now retired, who feels there is a cleansing effect of letting it out, a kind of renewal; he sees anger as a "good, wholesome human experience." More typical is a conditional sharing. A young man in his twenties says he is more likely to share his anger feelings with strangers or acquaintances, but with friends he tends to hold it in longer until it crosses a line. When angry at his girlfriend or his parents, he usually walks away and "takes it out on a wall or something" and then returns to talk with them when he's calm. Another says he is much more inclined to talk it out with someone today, though whether he does depends on the circumstances. For example, if it seems as if nothing will be gained from sharing his anger, he is unlikely to approach the person. Another "lets it go" if it's personal and not done out of malice. Several men mentioned that they were most likely to share their anger feelings with those close to them but not typically with those they do not know well.

Of those who expressed anger in an open and explosive manner when they were growing up, almost all have been working on changing their ways. Only one is still fairly spontaneous and open with his anger, though he is not as physical as he used to be; he expresses his anger openly and gets over it and feels better. Although he dislikes anger situations (because they "break the harmony"), he believes it's all right to get angry as long as one is not hateful or malicious.

Over and over I heard men contrasting earlier behavior with current behavior. As one put it, "I would blow off at the mouth, throw punches, grab, and apologize later." As a child, he said his anger intensity was a 100; later it decreased to a 90; and today it's a 30, and he is working to get it down even further. His patience has increased, and he is excited about changing his and his family's attitudes and behaviors regarding anger and feels that his whole family is working together toward that goal.

Some have been motivated to change by a particular incident in their lives. One young man recalls that he and his father would get into tense, angry confrontations from time to time. After his father's death, this young man went through a stage of destructive anger episodes where he kicked, hit, and broke things. This destructive wave came to a halt the day he broke his finger after "hitting something that didn't move and I realized there had to be a better way." Today he says it takes a lot to get him angry; he may start to yell but then realizes that he better cool down before things get out of hand. He vividly remembers his past and realizes that his anger style left a lot of scars—and not just on his finger.

Another male, who is now age fifty, said that as a preteen and early teen he had a violent temper. One particular time he got extremely angry over an incident with his father; as a result of this experience he thought for hours and hours and decided he would never again be in a situation where he was not in control. Today he is still fearful of his anger and of being pushed beyond control; rather than risk losing control again, as he did many years ago, he now leaves the situation. Later, he will come back and talk about it if it's needed. A third man, now age fifty-three, also had "very much of a temper" as a young man but learned to control it when he went to work selling cooking utensils and learned that he could not always express what he felt.

For many of the men, age, maturity, the help of a spouse, the influence of religion, and a decrease in stress contributed to adopting a calmer style of dealing with conflict. One man, now fifty-three years old, compares his behavior today to twenty years ago and states that back then if he had been in a traffic altercation, he would have felt obligated to respond and to defend his ego or manhood, but today, he'll let it go and figure, "This is just a damn fool anyway!"

Today, the great majority of the men say they are comfortable (to one degree or another) with their own anger. Only three say that they are not. One of these admits that his way of dealing with things is probably not always physically healthy. He suffers from severe back problems and because he believes that physical and mental aspects are interrelated, he worries that he is not dealing with stressful situations well. A couple of men either were not sure if they were comfortable or said it depended on the situation. One elderly white male who is now retired recalls that when he was younger, he had no idea of how to deal with the emotions. He spent some time in the military service and found that most people there yelled, gestured, and cursed when angry. This was not appealing to him. Later he realized how important it is to be able to understand, evaluate, and determine proper methods of dealing with feelings. He now goes through a mental process where he evaluates why he feels the way he does and diffuses it. Although he describes himself as being "very comfortable" with his own anger, he is not yet where he'd like to be. On occasion he still blasts out at others before his process works, and he's always ashamed within ten seconds after the fact.

Fewer men are comfortable with others' anger than with their own. About half of the people interviewed feel comfortable when anger is directed at them. For many, it varies with the situation or person. For example, one man can accept another's anger only when that anger is grounded in a logical basis; otherwise he has problems with it. Another man is less comfortable when the situation involves a friend than when it's a stranger. One man, who is very comfortable with his own anger, says that he is not uncomfortable but concerned about others' anger because the majority of people don't have the knowledge and ability to reason out their own anger process and thus may not know how to control anger. He knows anger can be dangerous.

Several of the men have developed interesting and useful ways to look at anger situations. One middle-aged man, who used to be quite temperamental and underwent a lot of emotional trauma during childhood, now has this philosophy: "If you get angry with me, I need to go to you and say something like, I know you're mad at me, but I don't feel any differently about you. Everything is all right!" He believes that if you care about someone, then you don't want the other to have negative thoughts, and thus it is our duty to initiate interactions with love. He thinks that there are people who have literally set off bombs (destroying lives and property) because nobody ever said something loving and forgiving to them. An elderly man in his sixties admits that in his younger years he had no idea of how to deal with his emotions, but over the years he learned to use a mental process of evaluation and diffusion. He firmly believes that anger needs to be expressed. He has learned to think of anger in terms of a fire:

It's a wonderful emotion if you can imagine it in terms of fire as used in a barbeque grill. One can take the control knob and turn it down or slightly up in order to accomplish something that is worthwhile. On the other hand, if one allows anger the latitude as in a forest fire, it is completely out of control and sometimes consumes thousands of acres. That's the way I view anger. That it has the potential for both points there and we as people, if we could keep in mind that anger is something appropriate when under control and used, but it also can be very devastating to the individual and those people around it. If it's ever let loose enough to cross that line, it becomes out of control.

Frequency of Anger, Women and Men

All were asked about how often they get angry in a month. This anger was not tied to gender-related issues. Responses were grouped into three categories: rarely (twice a month or less), sometimes (between three and five times a month), and a lot (more than once a week). Some respondents qualified their remarks. For example, one woman who said she gets angry four to five times a month stressed that this refers only to significant others, because with strangers she gets angry on a daily basis. About equal numbers of women fell into each of the three categories.

Almost all of the men ended up in the "rarely" or "sometimes" category (with more in the "rarely" category), with only one man saying he got a angry "a lot." One man said he "never" got angry. One man refused to give a frequency because, as he put it, "Sometimes things rock along just fine, and other times there's a lot of situations that create anger." Another man expressed the opinion that it varies a lot; one month he'll be angry a lot, and the next month he doesn't get angry at all.

The biggest sex difference occurred for high levels of anger, with more women getting angry "a lot" than men. One woman said that sometimes she has been angry "for months at a time!" Another recalled that it used to be that "there were not numbers high enough" to describe how often she got angry in a month. Just recently this woman has been making drastic changes in her anger style with the help of a therapist.

Quite a few of the participants hesitated when they were asked how often they got angry in a month because they were trying to make distinctions between what some called "anger-anger" or "really angry" and "irritated-angry" or "frustrated-angry." It was clear that if one used the latter definitions, their levels of anger would have been much higher. Many of them saw anger as something that was strong enough to put them in a "rage" or as something associated with losing control. If they raised the question, they were urged to think of being "angry" rather than just "annoyed" or "irritated."

Targets of Anger

When asked, "At whom do you most often get angry?" there was more congruence than difference between the women and men. Both sexes named their spouse or ex-spouse and then their children (primarily sons) as the two most common sources of anger. It was interesting that children were a very close second to wives or husbands; in other words, these men and women got mad at their children almost as often as they got mad at their spouses. Several individuals expressed much more frustration and anger in reference to their children than in reference to their spouse. One man said that he got mad more often at his daughter than anyone else and that what drove him crazy was that she will not let him finish before "getting in his face" and challenging him. He does not know how to handle such disrespect without losing his cool. Another man talked about how he used to be much calmer but that in the last few years he has become "an angry man" due to problems caused by his son.

The third most commonly mentioned source for women and men were work-related individuals; women called them "coworkers" and men referred to bosses, employees, and coworkers. For men, these individuals tied with "myself" as targets of anger. The fourth most common target of anger for females consisted of family members other than spouses (parents or siblings). Other people were mentioned only once by either women or men.

BELIEFS ABOUT SEX, GENDER, AND ANGER

Two questions were asked about the influence of a person's sex on anger expression. (Those interviewed in the very beginning were not asked these questions.) The first question asked whether the other person's sex (being male or female) made a difference as to whether or how respondents expressed their own anger. Women and men answered this question very differently; about one-fourth (six) of the women and two-thirds (fifteen) of the men were convinced that sex makes a difference in their own anger expression.

The relatively few women who felt sex was an important variable were split as to which sex was easier to share anger with; two said it would be easier to share feelings of anger with a woman, and three indicated they would be more likely to talk to a man. One woman said the difference was that men tend to make her angry a lot more than women do. One woman noted that she kept her feelings hidden from men. Even when her husband had an affair for three years, she kept feelings inside and kept living with her anger until she reached a breaking point and ordered him to get out. If she was mad at a woman, she would have no problems telling her. She added that her therapist attributes this pattern to her negative relationship with her stepfather.

Another woman mentioned that she generally trusts women more and thus can share anger feelings more easily. A young, unmarried mother of two exclaimed, "Sex makes a big difference!" She makes friends more easily with men and doesn't really trust women. When she gets mad at a woman, she says she will be mad at her for the rest of her life, but when she's angry at a man, she gets over it much more quickly once he apologizes. She also gets angry at a woman much more easily than a man. As she put it: "A woman can do *anything* to make me mad! Just her being beautiful makes me angry." Another respondent finds it easier to talk to men when angry because she sees men as less emotional, more logical, and easier to talk to. The other woman who found men easier to talk to said it was because she has been around more men than women. However, she tended to find men more intimidating than women. She seemed ambiguous about the situation.

The majority of the female respondents felt that the other person's sex was not an important variable in their expression of anger. These women believed that other things, such as the individual's personality, the rapport between them, the power of the person, or how close they were to the person, were much more important determinants of whether or how they shared anger. As one would expect, they were more forthcoming with their real feelings with individuals whom they were closer to, had less power over them, and were receptive and kind than other individuals. One woman mused that although personality is a more important factor in determining whether she would share feelings of anger, sex is a factor in the sense that women make it easier for people to express emotions. With men, she thinks, there is the fear that sometimes they won't control their anger and thus may storm off or drive off squealing their tires, thus making it very difficult to continue a discussion.

Unlike the women, the majority of the males felt that the other person's sex does make a difference. "Oh, heck, yeah!" said an older gentleman in response to this question. "I have learned to realize and understand that in everything in life, sex makes a difference." Of the men who think sex is an important factor, more than half said they would change their style of expression with a woman. They would be more indirect, more gentle, less loud, less harsh, less open, more careful, more restrained, and more patient. These men were afraid of hurting women's feelings or offending women's sensibilities. One man referred to his own wife, who "breaks down easily" when he tells her how he really feels, and thus he has learned not to tell her a lot of his strong, negative feelings. One man said he would get angry more quickly with a female than a male, especially a female who questioned his abilities or judgment. Several would be less likely to express any anger to a female. Only two males felt that they would be more open and would find it easier to talk to women about their anger than men. One male said that although sex is not that big a factor, he would be more careful with a big, strong male because such an individual might fight him; he feels more relaxed and open with women (and they tend to be weaker physically) and thus he might be quicker to say something to a woman when upset.

Although proportionally fewer males than females believed that sex made no difference, those who did gave answers similar to the women for what does make a difference. Basically, men also identified the level of closeness and the personal attributes of the other person as the two most important factors. Although the pattern was similar to the women's, one young man said that what mattered most was people's attitude toward him; if they were friendly and nice toward him, then he would be less likely to share his anger with them. Most of the other respondents found it easier to share anger feelings with such individuals.

These findings imply that when women are angry, they are less likely to moderate their response based on the other's sex but will be more sensitive and attentive to personal and relationship characteristics. Generally, the closer the relationship and the friendlier the person, the more likely they are to express their feelings. For males as a group, the sex of the other is a much more salient characteristic when it comes to anger expression. Unfortunately (or perhaps fortunately) a woman is less likely to hear of his anger feelings unless other characteristics mitigate the fact of her sex. On the other hand, *if* he expresses them, he will be more restrained, more indirect, and more patient.

Respondents were also asked whether men and women are different when it comes to any aspect of anger. Almost all the women who were asked this question (nineteen out of twenty-two; three women were not asked this question) believed that there are differences between the sexes; only three said that sex has nothing to do with it. The pattern was almost identical for the male respondents, with the overwhelming majority (twenty) believing that women and men are different and only three believing that they are the same. One was not sure (one was not asked).

Women's Perceptions

Women's beliefs varied widely. In regard to who is more open and who holds anger in more, the women were divided, with equal numbers believing that men show anger more and equal numbers thinking that women show it more. In response to the question, one woman said, "Definitely! Men are more volatile and open; women tend to hold anger in." A middle-aged, professional woman said with great conviction:

Absolutely! Men are much more direct. They feel that they have the right to be; that it's okay to be. So they can be much more direct. They can call you an "asshole" straight to your face and be done with it and go on. Women are much more [she pauses] I don't know if they feel a need not to express it because it's not feminine or whatever. But they use different tactics of expressing anger, very much behind the back, around the corner, up and down, and through someone else and you never know what's going on. You don't ever know if this person is really angry at you or angry at something you did, something you didn't do. If they're really, really angry. Because if you go back to them and ask them they say, "Oh, no, everything's fine!" So that has been my experience with the differences between men and women. I've had some head on discussions and very politely called a guy an asshole and he agreed and then called me the same thing very calmly and professionally. The next day we went out to lunch, you know.

A couple of people qualified their remarks and said that men were more straightforward *only* with other men, and not with women. Women were seen as quieter, more passive, more indirect, and having a harder time expressing such an emotion. One woman, who believed that women keep anger inside and get depressed, put it this way: "Men get mad; women get sad." Along with this view of women was voiced the idea that women tend to draw anger out much longer than men do; "some pout and pout and pout!" Men's anger typically was seen as more short-lived though more volatile.

Five women felt that men hold their anger inside more and are quieter and more controlled than women; they are reluctant to show it openly. Just as convinced as those who believed otherwise, a woman said bitterly, "Men won't say anything and keep it inside." She talked about how "men don't know how to communicate" and that her ex-husband was mad at her for four years; she didn't have a clue until one day he came home and wanted a divorce. One woman recalled her father who would not talk about why he was angry, but over time the family realized that he was angry whenever he came home and cleaned the house. A young black woman stated that a woman wants to be heard when she's angry; she wants to let it out and talk about it, while a man is usually quiet and doesn't want to be bothered. She also believes that men are more likely to run away from their anger, while women tend to confront it. She attributes this to a lack of maturity, citing her own boyfriend who left when she got pregnant.

Opinions were also expressed as to the nature of the anger expression. Almost all who addressed this dimension believed that men are much more physical and violent, less controlled, and more aggressive in their expression of anger. A few respondents saw women as more vocal, impulsive, and louder than men.

A few of the answers were along different lines. One woman said that men are very selfish and have high expectations of others; if they are angry, they will be more concerned with their own feelings than those of others. In a related vein, another woman felt that women make it easier for people to express their emotions; they make more space for the venting of emotions because, unlike with men, there is no fear that they won't control their anger. Men are perceived as being more likely to lose control and storm off, thus making it hard to continue a discussion of the problem. A couple of women said that women are more understanding and forgiving than men when it comes to anger.

Men's Perceptions

Just like the female respondents, the majority of the male respondents believed that women and men are different when it comes to aspects of anger. Only three felt there were no differences. One of these men qualified his answer by saying that if we could inject people with sodium pentothal and they would be completely honest, then there would be very little difference between women and men. However, because of socialization, women tend not to express anger as much and women are more forgiving.

The men in this sample were less divided than the women about who is more open and who is more reluctant to share anger feelings. Out of those who addressed the issue of hiding or sharing anger feelings, three times as many men believed that men are the more open and direct sex. Said one, "Men are brought up to express anger and deal with it more openly; women are asked to be meeker and quieter and more indirect." A middle-aged man thought that girls in our society learn that "good girls don't feel anger and should never feel it." Boys, on the other hand, are taught that anger is good and macho. Anger is a drive, he said, and boys misinterpret this and think that anger is desirable. He also sees men as less thoughtful and more "brutish and caustic" and thinks that men learn that anger is to be expressed only with those who are weaker, subordinate, or inferior. A couple of men felt that women have a tendency not just to be quiet and indirect but to be "manipulative" and "sneaky." Only a few men felt that females are more outspoken and open about their anger feelings while men hide their feelings because it is the macho, stoic thing to do.

Other contrasting views of men and women were expressed. Some said women were less rational and logical, and some said they were more rational than men. Various other beliefs were expressed too. One was that women won't let the anger situation be an issue of discussion that can be dealt with, but instead keep beating an issue and want to keep talking about it. Another felt that women are more likely to make judgments in anger and that these last a long time because "it's deeper emotionally for women than it is for men." Several men believed that women have a better handle on or insight about most emotions than men and understand what is happening to them better than men do. One man who made this last point elaborated and claimed that women need what he called "soak time," or time to figure out what is happening emotionally. He said that men usually call this time "sulking." One middle-aged professional man felt that men tend to put up with things until they explode, while women's "hot button" is further down, and thus they let it out faster and avoid the buildup of anger followed by the explosion. He also believed that women's friendship networks allow them to discuss problems and relieve pressures. He sees the typical man as not having access to such a safety valve. This man has now joined a group of men who meet regularly, and it gives him a chance to air troubles and concerns in a supportive context. He is enthusiastic about it!

In summary, men are much more likely than women to believe that the other person's sex makes a difference to them in regard to expressing their *own* feelings of anger. The women seem to be more attuned to the personality characteristics of the person or the relationship status. For males, the fact of femaleness or maleness is more salient (particularly the fact of femaleness). Almost all of the males who said sex is a factor seemed concerned about overwhelming, hurting, or offending a female. There was little concern when the interaction partner was a male because they felt that men could take it or would understand. The presence of males was not usually seen as problematic in the sense that they could be "themselves" with them and say it as it was. Although men and women shared the view that men and women are different when it comes to aspects of anger, they did not agree on how differences manifest themselves. The women split on the question of openness versus holding anger in, with half feeling that men are more outspoken than men and the other half believing that women are more likely to share anger openly. The majority of the men who addressed this issue saw men as the more outspoken ones. This perception is consistent with what men themselves say of their own anger expression, which is that they are more comfortable speaking to males than females.

SUMMARY AND CONCLUSION

In comparing men's and women's experiences, patterns converge and diverge. Both groups had childhoods that typically lacked consistent, specific, and constructive anger teachings. Although more women than men remembered being talked to about anger, most individuals of either sex lacked such discussions. Very few individuals remembered learning anything useful and constructive, but those who did found the learnings extremely helpful. Many individuals were exposed to a lot of anger in their interactions with family members, especially fathers. It is clear that the parents' behaviors and attitudes made a profound impression in either a negative or positive direction on many of these individuals. Many of the female respondents modeled themselves after their mothers, who more often than not hid their anger. In the few instances where both the mother and father had explosive tempers, the women tended to adopt a loud, explosive, and aggressive style themselves. More males than I had expected grew up holding their feelings of anger in. Perhaps the fact that so many had openly angry, hostile, and hot-tempered fathers discouraged anger displays on their part. Fathers who exhibited a lot of negative emotion did not always act to squelch angry outbursts in their sons. Several men with such fathers were extremely explosive and expressive themselves. One man recounted how, after a particularly big clash with his father, he left home at the age of sixteen and lived on his own. This man learned to control his formidable temper only after he tried to earn a living and found that an unbridled tongue was a quick way to lose customers.

The majority of women and men were unhappy with the modes of anger expression they adopted while young. Most seem uncomfortable with reactions at either extreme—holding anger inside or venting it explosively—and are in the process of moving away from these poles if they had been there previously. Relatively few are either very uncomfortable or very comfortable with their own anger today; most are somewhere in the middle. Fewer individuals are comfortable with others' anger than their own but slightly more male respondents than female respondents say they can deal well with others' anger.

Men and women report getting angry at the same type of people: spouses, children, and coworkers. Only after the top three targets of anger do they diverge. In regard to anger frequencies, patterns vary for male and female respondents. The women in the sample were much more likely than males to say that they get angry "a lot." This is consistent with research.

In expressing feelings of anger to others, women perceive themselves to be influenced by personal and relationship factors more than the person's sex. In contrast, most male respondents said that they modify their style of expression based on the other's sex. Both men and women agree that other women and men are different in their anger styles.

These findings make it clear that socialization practices in regard to anger and conflict-handling styles need to be reexamined. If the experiences cited by this group of individuals hold true for the larger population, we are not preparing people to deal with one of the most powerful and potentially destructive emotions of them all. The effects of the lack of learning or of modeling destructive ways of handling anger are long-reaching and long-term.

Chapter 6

Sources of Gender-Based Anger

A major goal of this project was to gain insight into what angers ordinary women and men about the other sex as well as their own sex and what they perceive to be other people's sources of gender-based anger. Although some research indicates that essentially men and women get angry about the same things, it is reasonable to assume that there are differences when anger is limited to the context of gender. Male and female subcultures have conditioned individuals to be different along many dimensions, and thus they are likely to have different goals and expectations and therefore what disappoints and angers them will probably differ too. Even if men and women share the same relationship goals such as understanding, respect, and equality, it is likely that each sex will attach different meanings to these objectives and use different strategies to achieve them, thus generating misunderstanding, frustration, and possibly anger.

When describing what made them angry about others' attitudes or behaviors, respondents were asked to distinguish between men and women they "knew personally" from women and men "in general." This distinction was made because it seemed reasonable to assume that the list of anger sources could differ for these two reference groups. One may get angry at one's husband or boyfriend for very different reasons than one gets angry at men as a group. One could be married, for example, to a kind and sensitive and feminist man who would never invoke his spouse's ire by being condescending, and yet his wife could regularly get angry at other men for such behavior. I wonder whether some of the more sensational gender-based anger reported in the mass media is a result of how people feel about men and women "in general." (Some of the individuals I interviewed had a difficult time with this distinction. They seemed to work from the inside out; thinking of people they knew as a basis for generalization to men or women in general.)

Respondents were also probed about their perceptions of what angered other men and women; this will be referred to as generalized anger. Although some said that they really had no idea, most (especially the female respondents) had definite opinions on what made other men and women angry at each other. What we think goes on in others' lives may be an important factor in the shape of our own discontent. It surely is harder to be satisfied with our position in society if we think that others like us are dissatisfied and frustrated. By examining the answers to these questions as well as earlier ones, we can answer whether men and women perceive same-sexed others to have the same concerns as their own. We can also see whether people's perceptions of what makes the other sex angry match what men and women say angers them personally. We can thus ascertain the extent of misperception that may exist between the sexes. It could be that women and men think that most men are upset about women working outside the home, but in fact very few men say this angers them. Such information is helpful in reducing feelings of anger and frustration.

The following section presents male and female respondents' sources of anger in reference to men and women they know and in reference to men and women in general. Since these involve their own feelings these sources of anger will be labeled personalized.

CROSS-SEX, PERSONALIZED SOURCES OF ANGER

What Angers Women About Men They Know Personally?

In response to being asked what angered them about the men they know (or specific men in their lives), several themes emerged as the dominant causes of anger for most of the women. Lack of responsibility and maturity angered more women than anything else. Women strongly denounced men who are "not taking any responsibility for earning money," "don't take care of their families," and refuse "to take responsibility for fathering a child." Other examples of irresponsible and immature behaviors were "not doing what they say they are going to do," "being lazy," not being on time, and not picking things up. Several women also felt that men were not responsible in regard to themselves and mentioned getting angry when a man "won't do things to help himself," or at men who are "not taking care of their own health" or "engage in self-destructive behavior" (such as drinking too much). Although some women were referring to irresponsible acts committed by sons and fathers, most had husbands or boyfriends in mind.

The second most common theme involved domineering and controlling behaviors on the part of men. One young woman said that her husband knows just how to control her, and he commonly does it by telling her (when they have a disagreement), "You just ain't never growed up." He automatically assumes that she can't have a valid point of view because he is older than she is. This same young woman also has a father who is domineering and critical and "pulls you down to get what he wants." Another young woman recalls her ex-husband telling her, "Now, you're just not using good sense. You need to go back and think about this some more." She did, and divorced him. These women talked about men who give orders, expect the women in their lives to change their views, give ultimatums, and manipulate them for personal gain. They deeply resent such behavior and expectations.

Another set of responses clustered around selfish, uncaring, and insensitive actions and attitudes. Examples of such behaviors were "saying you're going to do something and not doing it even though he knows it really bothers her," thinking that "everything revolves around them," minimizing her feelings by making decisions without consulting her, being critical of children from a former marriage knowing this really bugs her, not being there to give support, and walking out on her when she is mad at him though he knows this infuriates her.

This source of anger was followed closely in frequency by communication problems and superior, condescending attitudes. Examples of communication-related problems that angered women were "not knowing how to communicate with family members," a husband's pouting and refusing to tell her what upset him, being misunderstood by a spouse, and the inability or lack of desire to communicate. Several women were also upset by men in their lives (spouses, lovers, brothers) who conveyed that they're better than women or try to make them feel stupid, or discount their intellect.

Being sexually used or abused, men's overemphasis on sex, and lack of fidelity upset several women. One woman said in exasperation, "The only thing on their mind is sex!" A few women also mentioned inconsistent behaviors and expectations as sources of problems. One woman was perplexed by her boyfriend's behavior because one time he wants to be around her all the time, and then he wants her to leave him alone more. Another woman felt that she was damned if she did and damned if she didn't; nothing seemed to please him. Still another was frustrated by men holding a double standard so that if a woman does it, it's wrong, but if a man does it, it's all right.

A number of other complaints were mentioned more than once but not more than two or three times: lying, sexual harassment at work, having different goals (his not wanting to do what she wants to do), and being rigid about the male role. Mentioned only once were the following behaviors: being gullible, a son not having enough ambition, not listening (son), and a father getting too angry about politics.

The results of the interviews show that four of the five most commonly mentioned sources of anger in these women's lives are behaviors and attitudes that are directly tied to negative aspects or stereotypes of the traditional male role. Traditional conceptions of the nature of and privileges associated with gender allowed men (perhaps encouraged them) to be dominant, aggressive, sexual, superior, and uncommunicative (the strong, silent type). Women clearly do not find these attributes acceptable; they resent men who are controlling, insensitive, uncommunicative, and condescending. The large number of women who are angry about domineering or controlling and condescending behaviors indicates that women no longer see such behavior as a male prerogative.

Somewhat surprising was the prominence of irresponsible and immature behaviors and attitudes as sources of anger. Traditional masculine norms stressed the importance of being a responsible family man who thinks ahead and sacrifices for those he loves and those under his care. Many women in this sample are clearly troubled by the perceived absence of such traits. There are indications that individuals may be less willing to commit themselves to family roles today. Thornton (cited by Eshleman 1997) examined three decades (late 1950s through the mid-1980s) of changing norms and values in reference to American family life and found a weakening of the incentive to marry, stay married, have children, restrict intimate relations to marriage, and maintain separate roles for males and females. It may be that these women are picking up on this trend, and this is a theme of masculinity that they want to keep.

Much of the anger arises out of tensions over new expectations that women seem to have adopted. The fact that women get angry when men refuse to talk with them or display insensitivity attests to the importance that women place on caring, responsible, respectful, and open demeanor. That the men who engage in these behaviors are part of the women's lives and not "men out there" makes the situation that much more serious. Although the "modern" man is expected to develop these attributes, it is clear from the responses that he has a way to go.

Some of these women's complaints were echoed in the findings of a study of couples who had fallen out of love with their partners. Karen Kayser (1993) identified what she called "turning-point events"; of the twenty events, controlling behavior, lack of responsibility, and lack of emotional support were at the top of the list. Other problems, such as extramarital sex, physical violence, lack of self-disclosure, and sexual problems, played a less important role in falling out of love. There are indications that women in other countries share similar concerns. Japanese women, for example, were polled on their attitudes toward men, and they rated three-fifths of all young Japanese men as "unreliable." They also described them as self-centered, boring, predictable, and spoiled by their mothers (cited by Bird and Melville 1994).

What Angers Men About Women They Know Personally?

What was most striking about the men's responses to what women in their lives did to make them angry was the fact that no one type of behavior dominated. Men were angry about a wide range of behaviors, some of which were also cited by the women, but no particular behavior was mentioned by more than two or three men. There seemed to be little consensus among men as to what bothers them about women. The other notable difference was that four of the men said that "nothing" made them angry about the women they know. This did not happen even once with the women.

What is striking is that the responses generally do not mirror some of the concerns plastered across the front pages of magazines and newspapers or expressed in popular stereotypes. The men interviewed for this book do not have problems with domineering, uppity spouses or girlfriends or women who ran around on them or women who talk too much (with one exception on the last). It was interesting that of the three men who mentioned domineering, controlling behaviors, two of the three were referring to their mothers (not wives), whom they perceived as very pushy and controlling. One man called his mother a perfectionist who always told him to think about what "they" will think. He had to be the best in everything, "as though this would somehow make everything all right." Since one can never be perfect and failure was inevitable, he came to expect to be "dumped on." To this day, he struggles emotionally with a mother who continues to try to control and manipulate him even though he is now in his fifties. These men were angered by women who are rigid, insensitive, controlling, and talk too much (or too little); are deceitful, irresponsible, indecisive, and manipulative; won't trust them; are overly sensitive, messy, and late; and are angry at them. Each of these attributes was mentioned by two or three men. There were additional comments that were mentioned only once by a particular man.

Several of the problems mentioned refer to negative stereotypes of females in our society, such as being indecisive, manipulative, late, deceitful, or hypersensitive. These men clearly are not tolerant of "feminine games and wiles." Women in our society are supposed to be sensitive and caring, responsible, willing to share feelings and trust men. These men say they get angry when women don't live up to such expectations. Ironically, women get mad when men *do* live up to traditional expectations.

What Makes Women Angry About Men in General?

When the reference group was "men in general," the women most often mentioned men's condenscending, superior behaviors and/or attitudes. One woman said, "A large majority of them feel that women have inferior intellect, that we're not capable of thinking for ourselves. Where do they get this from? Who do you think took care of me before they came along?" Generally men who think they are superior to women in several different ways—who think they are "God's gift to women"—really bothered about one-third of the female respondents. A middle-aged homemaker said, "They'll put women down, but then they want them; men are just bad."

The next most commonly mentioned sources of anger were men's perceived overemphasis on sex and their abusive treatment of women. (The same number of women voiced these concerns.) "They're all pigs!" blurted out one young woman "They all want one thing, and that's a woman. They don't care what she looks like, how old she is. All men do it." Another accused men of thinking with their hormones instead of their brains. And a young divorced woman said, "The only thing they have on their minds is sex; that's all they have on their minds." Close to one-third of the women also talked about men's propensity for violence and abuse, along both emotional and physical lines. They were angry about rape, physical abuse, and men's competitive and aggressive style, which is hurtful to people. One woman lamented that men, more so than women, "seem to be so capable of hurting other people so badly and so often."

Men who are insensitive and selfish comprise another category of complaints. One woman expressed her sentiments using these words: "They think that everything revolves around them." Another woman said, "They tend to minimize the importance of a woman's feelings in relation to their own."

Women were also angry over work-related issues. One woman said she gets upset at men in general: "Mostly they think they work harder than women do." She insisted that women work very hard today and the more women do, the less men do. Men go to work, come home, eat, and go to bed; meanwhile, she has ten times more things to do. Another woman expressed a similar sentiment when she said that women have to work much harder than men. She also mentioned that women sometimes have to prostitute themselves in order to survive. Several other women resented the fact that although men may work hard for pay, they do not do their share of work around the house. A professional black woman was angry about what men perceive to be their male role: "I go to work and earn the money, and that's all I need to do; you take care of the rest." This woman added that she has seen changes between her husband's and his father's generation. For example, when her father-in-law wanted dinner, he tapped his fingers on the table; her husband would never do that. In fact, her husband is timid about asking what is for dinner.

One-fifth of the sample of women were angry at men for just "being men" or for sticking together because they're men. Said one, "They're men!" as though that needs no explanation. Another stated, "Men are just bad!" A couple of other women mentioned that they got angry and resentful over the way men "stroke each other" and justify each other's actions (even bad ones) and the way "they bond together." The bonding was not bad per se, but it made her angry that women couldn't do that. She noted that men will argue with each other one minute, and then watch a game together the next minute as though nothing had happened.

Several sources of anger were mentioned equally often, but only by a few women (three or four). One was men's perceived inability to think and communicate like women. As one woman put it, "Men don't think like women do; they don't have the same hard urge to communicate." Or another, "They don't know how to express their emotions as well as women do." Another woman was upset because men "don't take the same things as being important as women do." Another theme of anger was dominance. Several women were upset that men in general have "a controlling attitude" or "men who think that they can do to women whatever they want to do like construction workers who whistle."

Although irresponsible, immature behavior was the most commonly mentioned source of anger for men who were known, very few women found this to be a problem for men in general. One woman was angry about men not living up to their family responsibilities and simply said, "You're not a man when the court has to tell you to take care of your child."

Several other causes of anger were mentioned by the women, though these were given only once or twice. Among these were making light of sexual harassment, having affairs, holding double standards, being messy and disorganized, not telling the truth, and men's tendency to rank everything and then believe that their hierarchy is the best. One woman said, "I can't think of anything, I like men."

What Makes Men Angry About Women in General?

The top three sources of anger for men were lack of sensitivity, lack of responsibility, and deceitful or manipulative behavior on the part of women in general. A young man who works with teenaged boys and girls is angered by women who are insensitive to men and blame men for all the wrongs in their life. He believed that women need to realize that men are different. For example, men are more visual when it comes to sexual stimuli, and thus scantily clad women get their attention. When this occurs, the women call the men "perverts" for looking rather than realizing that this is typical male behavior. He also feels that if this type of behavior bothers women, they need to rethink their proclivity for dressing in sexually titillating ways. Another man gets very upset at women who make fun of their spouses in public situations such as a party. These women bring up things that, in his opinion, should be talked about in private. He admits that he used to belittle his wife in public over her messy housekeeping but has come to feel that this is disrespectful and has stopped. He continues to notice women who seem to relish the opportunity to cut their spouse down to size at parties or other public occasions. A lot of these husbands are "out there working their fingers to the bone while the wives are social butterflies who are playing; they're not in the trenches, and then they pick on their spouse at a party." He believes that this type of behavior is just as wrong when carried out by men.

When complaining about lack of responsibility, men mentioned such things as "never accepting responsibility for doing a wrong," the failure to address issues of right and wrong, failure to deal with a situation at hand, and women who won't take responsibility for having and properly taking care of babies.

An equal number of men were angered by manipulative and deceitful women. A middle-aged man whose job entails a lot of contact with women gets riled up over women who use their physical attributes to "maneuver a man into her corner," whether she deserves his support or not. "A beautiful face covers a multitude of sins," he states. A white, middle-aged man with a high-status career is very frustrated because women who deceive believe that it's not wrong! One woman told him, "It's part of my makeup." This encounter has influenced his thoughts about women in general. A business owner is troubled by women who take advantage of men, whether it's financial, sexual, or men's respect for women.

He talked about friends who are in their sixties and have gone through a divorce or have lost a spouse through death. Quite a few of these men are "being taken for a ride" by young women who are really after these men's resources but who feign love and concern.

The next most commonly mentioned source of anger on the part of the men was condescending or superior behavior by women. A man in his twenties resents women who exhibit the attitude, "You're a man. You're stupid!" He finds this attitude of superiority very troubling and says, "If women are busy fighting the battle that women are better and men are busy fighting the battle that men are better, then we're gonna stay right where we are, just fighting instead of working together and trying to press on and advance as a culture." A man who is near fifty is angered because "women believe that all men fit a stereotype." He hears a lot of women project stereotypes such as, "We know how you men are!" or "All men are dogs!" He feels that men are not as likely to make comments of a similar nature about women. He feels that women are not only putting men down but are also keeping men in a box by stereotyping them along rigidly defined masculine roles: "Because you're a male you're supposed to be the breadwinner."

Several men were upset by women who seemed to lack self-respect or a strong backbone. An older man who is now retired laments that women don't know how valuable they are. He feels that women have an incredible contribution to make to society and to relationships but that many women are not aware of their special powers and insights. A young man who was raised by his mother to respect and understand women gets angry at women who "serve men hand and foot." Other behaviors mentioned under this category were women flaunting themselves sexually and women who let themselves go physically.

Many issues were mentioned by only one or two men. A couple of men are angered by selfish, uncaring women, such as those who show up late and don't feel guilty. Other responses included fighting among themselves, women who sit at home doing nothing but watching TV all day, being unfaithful, being abusive, and women who want to be in the military. Only one man was upset by controlling women. He cited an example of a friend's wife who wants to have control over her husband at all times, even when she's not with him. For example, this husband may want to play golf with friends while she is getting her hair done, but she won't let him play and makes him stay at home alone. This same man, a young black male aged thirty-two, is very angry when it comes to women who lose their identity to men so that they have nothing outside of that man. An older man who owns and runs his own business gets upset because "women these days think anything is harassment." He talked about how "in his day" you could walk up to a woman at work and put your hand on her shoulder and that was okay. Today, according to him, a woman has free rein to bring up charges against men for the pettiest behavior, and then "the men are left to hang out to dry." Whether he's guilty or not, his character and career are damaged. Seven men couldn't think of anything that angered them about women in general. Some of these commented, "I don't get angry at women in general; I tend to hold women in high regard, generally speaking" or "I have no preconceived notions of anger or women." It was interesting that several additional men in their initial answer to the question said things like, "Nothing; I like women," or, "I can't think of anything; they're pretty slick," but then proceeded to list things that anger or upset them.

Later in the interview, respondents were asked about their general feelings in regard to changes in the roles of women and men, and as they answered this question, several other points of anger came out. In fact, the feelings expressed often were more vehement than when asked directly about what angers them about men and women. When discussing recent social changes, several men expressed their disgust with women who want equal pay and opportunities but are not willing to compete under the old conditions or standards. These men felt strongly about issues such as affirmative action and women in the military, and it was at this point in the interview that they seemed to get the most emotional and agitated. A fair amount of this anger was directed at the government, which they perceived as promoting unfair policies and interfering in personal lives in negative ways. In a sense, there was as much anger at the laws, the leaders, and the way organizations are structured as at the women who took advantage of things like affirmative action as well as those who agitated for changes in current standards.

Comparison of Cross-Sex Anger Sources for Both Reference Groups

Women are angry at men they know primarily because men are irresponsible, domineering, insensitive, noncommunicative, condescending, and sexually exploitative. They are angry at men in general because they are condescending, sexually exploitative, physically and emotionally aggressive, insensitive, treat them unfairly in regard to work issues, and because "they're men."

When men were asked what angered them about women, no one explanation dominated. Men listed many traits but had no consensus on what angered them about the women in their lives. Some of the sources of anger were the same as those mentioned by some of the women (being insensitive, domineering, irresponsible, and not sharing thoughts enough). Men are angry at women in general because they are insensitive, irresponsible, and deceitful and manipulative.

Lack of sensitivity was the one anger source that was mentioned by all respondents for both specific and general others. Lack of responsibility cut across men's and women's lists, though not as consistently as insensitivity. There were some sources of anger that were perceived by only one sex or the other. For example, only female respondents complained about sexually exploitative and obnoxious behaviors, only females listed physical acts of aggression, and only females complained about acts of laziness around the house. Only females said that "just being a man" was enough to elicit anger; no male uttered such a generalized sentiment. On the other hand, only males complained of deceitful, manipulative actions and attitudes.

There was some overlap for women's anger sources across both types of men. Although the complaint may be the same, the proportion of women who listed the same offenses sometimes varied from one reference group to the other. For example, slightly over one-third of the women listed insensitivity as an anger source for men they know, but only one-fourth listed insensitivity for men in general. Thus, although women's anger is aroused by many of the same behaviors in both groups of men, some of these are much more common sources of anger for acquaintances.

Women were much more likely to identify grievances for both groups of men. Only one woman said "nothing" made her angry (about men in general). Four men said nothing angered them about the women in their lives, and seven said nothing angered them about women in general. Why this is so is not clear. It could be that men truly are more content than women, or it could be that they were not willing to share their thoughts with the interviewer. Women's behavior is consistent with the view of women as the relationship experts in our society; in this role they are more likely to look for and notice when things are out of kilter. Goleman (1995) states that men have a "rosier" view of marriage and that wives are more "attuned to the trouble spots" as well as being more vocal about complaints.

SAME-SEX, PERSONALIZED SOURCES OF ANGER

What Angers Women About Women They Know Personally?

Not much research has focused on what angers individuals about their own sex. While I had the opportunity, I thought it would be interesting to explore the kinds of behaviors and attitudes of their own sex that anger women and men. Do similar actions anger us regardless of whether they originate from the same or other sex? Do people buy into stereotypes about their own sex?

When women thought about women they knew, what emerged as the most commonly mentioned source of anger was their lack of self-esteem and self-respect. Looking around at the women they know, the respondents were troubled and angered when women let themselves be abused and treated with disrespect, depend too much on a man, don't stand up for themselves, are insecure and jealous, and cater and kowtow to men. One young woman's sister always does what her husband wants to do regardless of her own wishes. The same woman has a friend whose husband works out regularly, but the wife (who is overweight) can't find the time to work out because she is responsible for the care of the children and the house. On the rare occasion that this woman does take time to exercise, she would rather ask a friend to pick up her children from day care than ask her own husband to do so.

One woman says she knows a lot of "together" women but has met too many others who make the same mistake over and over again, don't go forward, and drag others down with them. She sees this among educated women as well as those with little or no education, although more are represented in the latter group.

When she encounters a woman who has trouble being independent and strong, she tries to point things out to her if she is a friend or she sees her regularly. However, this doesn't always work out well. For example, she has a good friend who is married to an emotionally abusive man, and when this friend confided in her, she tried to be supportive and point out alternatives. Her friend decided to go back to this man and now will no longer talk to her about this situation. This has happened to her repeatedly. She now has decided to stay out of it.

Two related behaviors comprise the next most commonly mentioned sources of anger: sneaky, back-stabbing, untrustworthy women and manipulative and game-playing women. Many women used the word *back-stabbing* to describe the type of behavior that makes them angry about women they know. These women felt that they could not trust other women with confidences because they talked behind their backs, and were conniving. One woman said bitterly, "I thought she was my best friend, and she proved to be otherwise." A lot of women also saw other women as being manipulative and as playing games. "Women play too many games," said one. Examples of game playing were "who can outdress who," "playing dumb," "putting on the helpless act," and "making yourself a scarce commodity." Some were upset by women "using their body to get things" and women who fake love in order to gain financial security. One young woman scathingly denounced women who act as if they know nothing when a man comes around and, change their voice and attitude in his presence. She also despises women who complain about men to other women but as soon as a man enters their presence treat him as though he was wonderful.

Quite a few women (one-fifth) reached consensus on two other complaints: indecisiveness or weakness and superiority behavior. Under the first category fell such actions as "changing their minds a lot," "not taking responsibility for problems," "indecision," and "wanting to be independent, but when they can't do something they crawl back to a man." One woman expressed the opinion that women are not raised to take responsibility for problems or think for themselves. She urged women to realize that they can change and make new choices and be different. Another charged, "If there's a problem and it's been going on for a long time, why don't they do something about it instead of whining?" Women were also angry at other women who acted as if they were better than others and bragged about their position and accomplishments. One woman complained of women looking down on other women because they're not as rich or pretty as themselves. She thinks that men don't do this; men will find something that is shared in common, such as hunting or fishing, and thus make a connection. Another comments on how awful it is living in a small town where the women are extremely judgmental, treating her as though she is below them. Some statements referred to the work setting where women made sure that others knew they had the competitive edge.

A variety of answers were given by only one or two women. Petty, nitpicky behaviors, being treated like a child by a mother, sisters who say hurtful things, incompetence, not giving your best, and women talking about each other in a stereotyped way about how catty and hard to work for other women comprise many of the responses in this category. Two women said that nothing made them angry about women they knew.

What Angers Women About Women in General?

Two of the twenty-five women said that nothing bothered them about women in general. Based on the others' responses, the pattern for women in general was very similar to "women you know." The most consistent source of anger was again lack of self-esteem and respect. It angered the respondents that women are insecure and jealous, take things personally, won't stand up for their rights, and cater so much to men. One woman said that jealousy among women (over men or over attention other women are getting) made her angry and that women miss out on a lot of good relationships with other women because of this. A middle-aged, professional, very self-assured black woman stated emphatically that "women are their own worst enemy" because they do things to themselves that set them up for failure. She has seen women who, because of their low self-image, end up with men who are losers—not once but ten times. She knows women who have a wonderful job but are willing to give it up and move in order to be with a man. "As a gender," she says, "we are just not as strong and positive about where we are going as we need to be." This woman went on to talk about sexual harassment as an example of women's insecurity. Today she observes many women screaming about sexual harassment. She says she could have complained about it all the time in her work but never paid it any attention. She thinks this all goes back to self-image and what it is based on. You have to realize, she says, that people don't always say things that lift us up, and so we shouldn't tie our self-image to what other people say or do. "As women, we don't have that confidence; our self-image is wrapped up in things it shouldn't be, which is why we can be so catty, why we don't deal with problems straight on. We'll never have power until we deal with the basics [self-worth] and being independent and making decisions based on it."

As before with "women you know," the next two most commonly mentioned sources of anger were sneaky, catty, and untrustworthy behaviors and manipulative and game-playing behaviors. Women perceive other women to be sneaky, back-stabbing, and untrustworthy. "They'll mess with your man!" exclaims one. "They'll back-stab you faster than you can say it!" exclaims another. One woman said that for all she knows, men may be the same way; she *does* know that women are that way. A young mother of two feels that women are more back-stabbing and vicious than men, who are more upfront. She has been betrayed by many more women than men and feels that she cannot trust women, especially in female-female relationships. One elderly woman is angry that women don't keep confidences. "You can't trust a woman," she says flatly. "If you tell her something, she'll probably tell her best friend; that's one reason I would pay somebody." (She was referring to paying a therapist.) A large proportion of women saw other women as manipulative and hypocritical. "Women don't want competition and play games to get what they want," states one woman. Examples of game playing were using their sexuality and flirting to get something or playing dumb and getting someone else to do work for them. These types of behaviors drew great disdain from many of the respondents. "Women try to get away with a lot of crap. If they want something, they go crying to a man, and of course, he'll do it because he wants a woman!" snorts a young woman. Women were also seen as being hypocritical. "They [women] want to be liberated, but when they don't know how to do something, whom do they crawl to? A man!"

A few women see other women as irresponsible. They won't keep promises or are negligent when it comes to taking care of their children. One woman said that some women will buy themselves clothes before they buy things for their children. Whining, being petty, and complaining were disliked strongly by another few respondents.

The rest of the reasons given for getting angry at women in general, cited two times or fewer, included strong feelings about militant and bossy women. One woman claims that a woman needs to be feminine even when she's angry; she can't curse or "be loose with the tongue." This woman was born and raised in the South and believes that women set the standards in our society. Another woman gets angry at what she called "militant" women, which she defined as "women who don't like men and who try to be like them." She thinks these women do society a disservice because women and men are different and she resents it that these women are trying to do away with differences. These women man-bash; men don't know what to do and feel attacked all the time. "We're in this life together, and we have to make it work," she concludes. Women also got angry when women are rude and insensitive toward other women or men, are selfish, have affairs, exhibit superior attitudes, are not helpful to other women, have abortions, abuse children, are stupid and incompetent, do not bond like men do, and are too competitive.

A couple of women gave somewhat atypical answers. One got angry at women who take their husbands for granted and don't appreciate them. "Here he is, staying at home a lot, he doesn't run around, does what he can and yet these women complain." This respondent works in a setting where she deals with a lot of women and has been struck by the fact that so many "stay ill or irritable all the time." And for the most part, they complain about their husbands. A woman in her forties who works with lots of women and men is frustrated about "the fronts we put up": "It's hard to develop good, strong, free, accountable relationships (even with other women) because of the walls and perceptions, the shadows that we keep thinking we see or feel that keep us from being real honest." When I asked her what she meant by "shadows," she explained that these are expectations we think other people have. In fact, she says, others may not perceive this at all, so we are trying to respond and react on the basis of what we think they are thinking; what we perceive to be there may in fact not really be there. These "shadows" trouble her because they separate people as we react in response to what we think that shadow is doing.

Focusing on the main sources of anger, it seems there is a single standard of anger for women who are known and for women in general. The top three sources of anger were identical for both reference groups: lack of self-esteem; sneaky, catty, and untrustworthy behavior, and manipulative game playing. It is clear that women want and expect other women to have high self-esteem and respect, they want to be able to trust them, and they want other women to pursue their goals without game playing, lying, or using physical attributes. I did not sense that these women were simply responding to popular, though negative, stereotypes; they obviously had experienced many of these behaviors and attitudes in their personal and public lives. Their voices and faces reflected strong emotions as they talked about the lack of trust, the envy, the jealousy, the insecurity, and the inability to deal with things in a straightforward and honest fashion. In the context of the women's movement and its ideals of sisterhood, such findings are disturbing. If these feelings are shared by women throughout our society, they will undermine the formation of strong, trusting, respectful bonds between women.

What Angers Men About Men They Know Personally?

One-third of the men said that nothing made them angry about the men they knew. Interestingly enough, another third were upset about sexist attitudes and behaviors on the part of other men. They were bothered by men who "condone women's degradation," cheapen women sexually, order women around, don't listen to women, and stereotype women. One man used the phrase "me Tarzan, you Jane" to capture the idea of men being the dominant ones. Similar concerns (but by fewer respondents) were voiced in regard to how men treat other men. Several respondents resented superiority behavior in the men they know. One man was angry because "men always want to be better than the other." Others resent men for being too competitive or too authoritarian.

The rest of the complaints were shared by four or fewer men. One involved deceitful and manipulative behavior, though this anger source and the following ones were cited by only four men. Here men were accused of lying, manipulating others for personal gain, for taking advantage of others, and hypocrisy. Selfishness was reported by a few men as their source of anger. One man spoke movingly of a personal experience with self-centeredness. The assumption that his wife would need nothing else in her life besides him almost cost him his marriage. He is determined never to have such a lapse in selfishness again. A couple of men were troubled by men who interact with each other in shallow and defensive ways and force themselves and their wives into playing stereotypical roles.

Various other complaints came up only once. One man was upset at men who focus too much on sexual aspects in their relationship with women; another got angry at men who abuse their spouses; not taking a stand based on principle was another source of anger; men who have blind spots when it comes to women were another. This respondent was disgusted because the most intelligent men act like fools when they are infatuated with a woman. "Rude and crude" actions, intolerance, constantly changing one's mind, and not defining issues and dealing with them were also mentioned.

What Angers Men About Men in General?

Four men said nothing angered them about men in general—half the number who felt that way in regard to men they know. More than half of the men said they get angry at other men who hold disrespectful and sexist attitudes toward women. Over and over again, male respondents were intolerant and upset over males who see women as weak, "cheapen women physically," treat women with disrespect, feel superior to women, stereotype women, and expect women to serve them hand and foot. One young man said that disrespect for women "drives me crazy." Another said that he was raised by his mom, and she taught him how women like to be treated. One middle-aged man, in response to the question, said emphatically, "The fact that they're men! That they are still dominant and have such a hard time accepting women as equals."

The second most commonly given answer dealt with men's tendency to act in a superior, condescending, "I'm the top dog" kind of way. Almost half of the male respondents were angered by men who belittle others, act as if they know something when they don't, always want to be noticed and recognized ("They're egomaniacs!"), and exhibit an attitude of superiority. One young black man said it really got to him when men let him know that "mine is faster, better, and bigger than yours."

Violent and/or abusive and crude, rude, and insensitive men comprise the next two most commonly mentioned sources of anger, with slightly more men being upset about the first one. Although most of the men were upset by violent actions directed at females (rape, spouse abuse), some of the comments included brutal and antisocial behavior aimed at people in general. Slightly more than one-fifth of the men got angry at males who are self-centered, self-indulgent, and discourteous and who act as if they don't care about others.

Several men expressed concern about men who are crude (cursing) and obnoxious (getting drunk) and men's unwillingness to share honest feelings or "being disingenuous" with each other. A middle-aged man in a high-status profession talked with disdain about the "huffing and puffing" that goes on among his colleagues. Another man is troubled about men "guarded with their feelings." Ideally, he would like to see men be more gentle, loving, caring, and tender as well as strong. Being too defensive and too shallow concerned another respondent, who believes that women can share more deeply and personally with each other than men can. Another man spoke movingly about the role playing that he commonly sees among men. He believes that men (and women too) are taught from childhood on to play roles rather than be honest with their feelings. The roles we are locked into make us dishonest; we have to lie since we cannot say things that are inconsistent with our roles. "We've all gotten buried in this dungheap of lies—about who we are and what we are and where we ought to be coming from," he says with strong emotion. He thinks that a lot of anger comes out of the frustration of not being able to be honest.

Being irresponsible raised the ire for some of the respondents. A young black male gets angry when he sees men who don't take care of their children and family. He believes that this is a man's primary duty and that he would do anything to keep his family safe. A handful of answers did not fall into any particular pattern and were given by only one respondent. These involved behaviors such as stupidity, lack of a social conscience, and men not realizing that women need their own identity. Four men answered that nothing made them angry about men in general.

Same-Sex Comparisons

Several patterns emerged in reference to feelings of anger toward members of the same sex. Similar to cross-sex findings, men were much more likely than women to say that nothing made them angry. Although only two female respondents said nothing angered them about women they know and the same number for women in general, fully one-third of the men couldn't think of anything that angered them about the men they know, and almost one-fifth felt that way about men in general. It is not clear whether men like their own sex more than women do or whether they are simply less critical or less likely to become angry.

The major sources of anger were similar across reference groups. Women complained about similar offenses whether they referred to women they know or women in general. For both groups, they listed lack of self-respect or self-esteem, sneakiness, manipulation, and untrustworthiness as the major sources of anger. Indecisive and condescending actions were singled out for women they know but not for women in general.

For their major sources of anger, male respondents listed sexist actions and attitudes, condescension, violence and abuse, and insensitivity. Only sexist actions and attitudes cut across both reference groups. The rest of the anger sources were in reference to men in general. (For all categories I designate a source of anger as major by using the one-fifth criterion; at least one-fifth of the respondents must have listed the same kind of offense.) It must be remembered that one-third of the male respondents said nothing angered them about the men they know.

A final pattern was that when female respondents thought about what made them angry about other women, their comments centered on how women treat other women. They resented sneaky, back-stabbing, condescending actions aimed at themselves or other women. In contrast, several categories mentioned by male respondents reflect the way men treat women. For example, many male respondents were seriously aggravated by the way men do not respect women and by physical and sexual abuse and violence aimed at women. It seems that women are less worried about how other women treat men than they are about how women treat each other.

Do men and women get upset about the same kinds of things when thinking about same-sex others? No. There is some overlap, with both male and female respondents resenting condescending actions and attitudes. But other attributes are mentioned by only one sex. What angered women the most was the lack of self-esteem or self-respect in other women. This was not an anger source given by the men. A lot of men dislike sexism in other men; women were not angered by sexism in women. Men complained of abusive, violent actions and insensitive, selfish behaviors, but no women did.

How much overlap is there between what angers people about members of the same sex and members of the other sex? Collapsing people who are "known" and "others in general" into one category, it is obvious that a few behaviors seem to anger almost everyone: condescension, lack of responsibility, and insensitivity. A lot of sources of anger are sex or category specific. Lack of self-respect is a big source of anger for women thinking about other women, but is never mentioned when women think about men and is mentioned by only a few men thinking about women in general. We don't know whether women don't find low self-esteem in men or whether they see it but it doesn't make them angry. Sexually exploitative behavior is mentioned by women only in reference to men. Not pulling one's weight in terms of work to be done is cited by women only in reference to men in general. Problematic communication patterns are mentioned only when referring to members of the other sex and never in reference to one's own sex. This implies that each has an easier time talking to members of their own sex and each feels understood, confirming beliefs voiced by Tannen (1990), Gray (1993), and others about the the perils of cross-sex communication. They essentially see men and women as living in two separate subcultures, each with its own goals and strategies for reaching them. Sexist attitudes were a big source of anger for men but not for women. In another part of the interview, a couple of women indicated that they were troubled by "male bashing." I did not get the feeling that most women saw other women as keeping men down or belittling them. When women complained of condescending attitudes and behaviors on the part of other women, it was in the context of women putting other women down. Women did not single out manipulative behavior as a source of anger in reference to men, but they did in reference to women, and men described such behavior as anger producing in regard to both types of women and in reference to men. Each sex saw members of the other sex as more insensitive than members of their own sex.

Although four women said that nothing made them angry about either category of women, twelve male respondents felt this way about other men (the majority of these were in reference to men they knew). This could imply that men like their own sex better than women do theirs or simply that men are less critical or less willing to share their thoughts on these matters.

Framing it in a positive fashion, men want other men to treat women in a respectful, egalitarian, gentle fashion, and they want men to approach other men with less pretense, game playing, and insensitivity. Women want other women to feel good and secure about themselves and be trustworthy, direct, competent, decisive, and responsible. Women want men to be more responsible and less controlling; treat women as equals; be sensitive, communicative, and nonaggressive; and be less focused on sexual matters. Men want women to be more sensitive, responsible, direct, and open.

GENERALIZED PERCEPTIONS OF ANGER SOURCES

Respondents were probed about their perceptions of what makes others angry. What we think goes on in other people's lives probably is an important factor in shaping our own discontent. It is harder to be satisfied with our own position in society if we think that others who are like us are not. It at least raises questions in our minds as to how things are and should be in our lives. Although some claimed initially that they had no idea what makes men angry at women and vice versa, most ended up giving opinions on what make women and men angry at each other. By examining the answers to these questions as well as earlier ones, we get an idea as to whether men and women perceive other individuals as having the same concerns as their own. We can also see whether people's perceptions of what makes the other sex angry match what men and women say angers them. In other words, we can get a sense of the extent of misperception. It may be that women (or men) think that most men are upset about women working outside the home, but in fact very few men say this angers them.

Perceptions of Why Women in Our Society Are Angry at Men

Women's Views

All but one woman shared their thoughts about what men do to make women angry in our society. (The one did not know what makes other women angry.) Four major sources of anger were perceived to exist. Women thought that other women are upset and angry about men who are irresponsible, treat women unfairly in the workplace, don't understand and support women, and have greater privilege and power. Minor sources of anger (mentioned by only a few women) were infidelity and men's stupid and immature behavior. A few other miscellaneous reasons were also given by a handful of women (men are letting aggression out on them, women are not really angry at men as a whole but at a particular man in their life, men are unable to handle the emotional side of life, and they want men to spend more time with them).

Women were perceived to be angry about men who do not assume responsibilities or don't take them seriously enough. In this category of complaints, two themes seemed to reoccur. One focused on men who are poor parents either because they are unavailable (have left the women and children) or don't do enough to take care of their families. The other theme revolved around the men's unwillingness to help out and share household and child care duties.

One woman whose job entails talking to many women on a regular basis says that most women talk about how lazy men are, while the women have to be superwomen. He watches television, while she works. This woman believes that men are increasingly happy to let women do more and more.

Under the category of unfair treatment at work, the female respondents believe that women become angry upon realizing that men make more money and that they (women) don't get the recognition or access to resources that they deserve. They felt that men are actively preventing women from achieving their goals and that women are upset about having to *prove* that they're equal and about having to work extra hard. A woman said with vehemence that other women are angry, "Because they have to continue to put up with this garbage, like the lack of equality. We hear about the laws and being treated equally but that's a lot of lip-service, and we don't believe it!"

The female respondents also felt that other women would be angry because men do not support, understand, and communicate with them enough. The feeling was that men don't know what women want and that they often put women down. One woman said what angers women is "when men make women feel as if they are less of a person," and when men don't live up to women's expectations. Another believes that women feel that they get a raw deal and are putting more into the relationship than the men are. A black female put it this way: "[They are angry] for not being everything we want them to be, for not being able to be what we want them to be, for not being able to make commitments."

Male privilege and power were also seen as problematic for women in our society. Women get upset, said the respondents, because men have more freedom and still control women, women have less power, and "men get their way." One woman explained that women are raised to cater to men, so that even today, while women work for money, they still do the work at home. Now, however, they are resenting it. Another woman felt that women are "getting a bad deal all the way around and feel they can't do much about it." They are so powerless that they even feel that they need a man to change things.

Infidelity was cited as causing anger among women by several respondents. Men are unfaithful and thus can't be trusted. Their attitudes toward affairs as "just another notch on their belt" are bad; these affairs "devastate women, who take relationships with men more seriously."

One woman had an interesting observation about how women deal with anger over men. She said that there are a lot of women angry, but they get over it by complaining to other women. They often will not say what bothers them to the man in their life. That is how they save their relationship with men.

Men's Views

Men were asked about their perceptions of what makes women angry in regard to men. Almost one-fourth of the men (six) claimed that they could not answer such a question because they were not sure what made women angry. One man said, "I've never really thought about women being angry in general." Two men asserted that women are not angry at men in our society. Thus, almost one-third of the male respondents did not provide any answers to this question.

The men's perceptions overlapped the women's to a great degree, in that they also talked about lack of equality and lack of sensitivity and understanding. The men felt that women resent their slow economic progress, being treated as unequals, and feeling as if men are holding them back. One man recalled a domestic law case. The wife made twice the amount of money her farmer husband did, yet, the husband kept talking about "my house," "my car," "my truck," etc. When cross-examined, the lawyer asked how this man figured everything was "his" since his wife made twice what he did. The husband's answer to that question was, "I *let* her work." He thinks a lot of women are mad about this kind of attitude. Another man talked about how women feel oppressed and have to overcome this feeling. They are breaking free of roles but see men as keeping them from doing so. He does think that women blame men more than they deserve and that women need to take some responsibility for some of their problems.

Men are also seen as not appreciating women's contribution. Says one, "She brings home the paycheck and thinks he should be thrilled, and he walks around pissed off because he feels threatened." An older man talked about a female coworker who has worked at the same company as him for thirty years. She periodically points out that they he came to the company at the same time and yet he has advanced way beyond her (she has a secretarial position and he is vice-president and co-owner of the business). He thinks a fair amount of women are upset about this kind of situation.

Many male respondents also felt that women were upset over men's lack of sensitivity and understanding. Accordingly, these women are mad because they want men to be more sensitive to their needs, because men have a difficult time understanding and meeting the emotional needs of women, and because men "dump on them or disappoint them." One man thought that more than half of all the women are angry and they are "sad and disappointed because their husbands won't listen to them, are not available or won't validate them in positive ways." Here they are at age forty, he says, and they've spent twenty years with this guy— the best years of their life—and they are not fulfilled. He's more interested in watching a basketball game than listening to her. Another man felt that these women are not getting as much attention as they want because the men are too busy and won't talk to them. They want their husbands to be their friends but men want to do "guy things" with other men instead. "They'd rather watch a ballgame than hold hands or take a walk."

Another man mused whether women have a lower threshold for sensitivity but nevertheless feels that women are upset about men's lack of concern for them. He'll say he's going bowling and that he'll see her later, and he doesn't ask her to come along or whether she has a problem with his going bowling. A young man believes that women are angry because a lot of men are insensitive, but he also believes that a lot of women are insensitive as well, but in different ways.

Only a couple of male respondents thought that women were angered because they are controlled by men or because they are not the head of the household. The rest of the men gave several miscellaneous answers: women being angry over rape and violence, men leaving women after they got her pregnant and letting her carry all the responsibility, dashed expectations or unrealistic expectations, and being confused over equality and sameness. One man thought that women's anger is tied to the state of the relationship she is in with a man. When first in love, he can do no wrong; later, when he leaves, all men are pigs.

Perceptions of Why Men in Our Society Are Angry at Women

Women's Views

Three women did not know why men are angry at women. One woman asserted strongly that men are not really angry at women. Why should they be? According to her, they don't have much to fear and women are still taking care of the kids and doing all the extras. Nevertheless, she thinks that men are angry at other men and at their life situation, and they take this anger out on women.

The rest of the female respondents overwhelmingly believed that men are angry at women because they do not like and are threatened by women's changing roles, which lead to increased power and demands. Two-thirds of the women felt this type of situation was behind the anger. These men were seen as losing control and power, losing jobs and preferences, and getting "a raw deal." They cannot deal well with a wife or girlfriend who is more successful than he is and has made great strides, with women who hit men back when he hits them, with women who ask the men to help out with things other than earning a paycheck, with women who may not need men as much as in the past. Says one woman, "A lot of men are frustrated by changing roles. Their roles used to be clear-cut. More women in the workforce demanding equal rights makes them frustrated and unsure, and they are hiding this." Another woman thinks that men want control and get angry because they don't have it or don't have as much as they used to. She mentioned the high level of domestic abuse and violence as being an indicator of men's need to be in control.

Some women felt that men's anger grows out of confusion with women's changing roles. It is not so much that they are threatened by or resentful of the changes but that they are no longer sure what is expected. Men no longer have a precise definition of what a man is. A thirty-seven year old woman put it this way:

The men try to establish they're men and there is no definition, no precise definition of what it means to be men anymore. Uh, many years ago, you know, a man was supposed to go do his job, provide for his family, discipline the children, and be with other men. And it has changed so much where now a man is supposed to be tender and they're supposed to have all these female traits, you know. I think it's good that men learn how to nurture, but I think there is a big deal of confusion because if they get too soft then the women don't like them either. Then they're wimps! And so they really don't know what their role is and I think they're blaming women for being in that position.

One woman thought men might feel trapped and feel they can't meet women's expectations. She wonders if women's expectations are too high and feels that men and women need to talk about this. Another woman sees men struggling with male-female roles; they want women to be more traditional than many are willing to be. She does think that men can accept some of the changes as long as they are not in their own house. The men she works with, for example, can appreciate her liberated stance and the work she does, but they are glad not to be married to her!

Lack of support and understanding is one of the primary sources of anger listed for women, but it was not mentioned often as an explanation for men's anger. A couple of people felt that it wasn't so much that men are angry at women but that some men are just angry individuals, either because of bad experiences (they were abused as children or had a nasty divorce) or because they don't love themselves and can't handle anger. Finally, there were various one-time answers, such as women teasing men or not engaging in enough sex, or women's need to analyze every situation. This woman felt that women overanalyze and always want to talk things over and read meaning into everything.

Men's Views

Four men would not give an opinion; they did not know why men are angry at women. Among the rest, there was great consensus that a major reason is women's changing role in our society.

There were several variations on that theme. One had to do with men feeling threatened in an economic sense. They assumed that men are afraid of losing their jobs to women or that they cannot handle the influence that comes with her paycheck. Some men are perceived to be angry because women are no longer as submissive to men or dependent on them, and they don't do what men want them to do. One man said men are angry "because of the times we live in." Men are threatened by women because they compete for jobs and are more aggressive than in the past. Another variation involved men's frustration with unclear roles. One man thought that men "feel invaded"; women are taking their places and forcing men to change their roles. Some men are perceived to be angry over women moving into places and positions "they have no business being in" and being too "pushy" about equality. A business owner and manager feels strongly that there are some jobs that women can't do or shouldn't do, and he believes this sentiment is shared by many other men. He and other male respondents believe that men and women are equal in some ways but not in all. They feel that the women's movement overdid it. Says one, "Some of these feminist groups feel that everything in the world has to be equal. There *are* basic differences between men and women, such as men being stronger as a group and women being more compassionate and nurturing." Thus men are strongly against women being in the front lines in the military and women and men sharing close living quarter in the military. Another sore point that several respondents mentioned had to do with the government's instituting programs like affirmative action and forcing businesses to redo work standards so that women can meet them.

In a related vein, some men felt that men in our society are angry because women want things but are not willing to work for them or don't appreciate what they have. One man said that what made men angry are "women who want an equal share of everything but are not willing to put forth an equal share of effort." Other men are perceived to be mad at women who now have "male" jobs, such as working at the United Postal Service, but complain about them. They were clear that men are angered by women who get the same pay as men but are not doing the same work. If a man and a woman are both traveling salespeople, and he is willing to be gone five days a week and she is not, then she should not get the same money. Another man feels that a lot of men are fed up with affirmative action and that women should be offended by it too. To him, affirmative action says, "You're inferior to me, and we've got to give you an advantage." Women should be offended, but they want something for nothing. He feels strongly that one has to work for an advantage, that it shouldn't be given, and that people have to make choices. To illustrate the latter point, he shared the story of a female friend. She is part of a professional couple who has lived together for seventeen years. Her position was that she would get married if they ever had children. She is not sure whether she wants to have children but says that *if* she did, she'd have to be willing to make sacrifices and that she would not be able to do her job the same way if she was a mother and that she would not be able to take care of her children properly if she continued to work as she does now. She feels that if she isn't around to raise her own children, why have them? So far she has opted for being a career woman. This woman is against affirmative action because she doesn't want people to say that she got the job only because she's a woman instead of her competence.

A few individuals thought that men are angry because there is not enough understanding between men and women, primarily because the sexes are just too different. "The sexes have different priorities," says one. "I think that men have a hard time understanding the priorities that women have, and that frustrates them because you can't see eye to eye." Another thinks that men feel misunderstood by women, although he puts the blame on the men for not taking the time to talk to their spouses; nevertheless, they get mad when women don't understand them. It doesn't help that women don't express their feelings and thus men can't know what they think and feel. This lack of understanding causes frustration and anger.

Another minority view was that women are scapegoats. They thought that men use women as a crutch for justifying their own actions and failings and then blame women. Another thought that the majority of men are angry with life in general (their jobs, feeling that things are unfair), and women become a convenient focal point. They are not the cause of the anger, but most men do not realize this.

A couple of men thought it's not what the women do; it's just that some men are angry people with hostile personalities.

A large number of miscellaneous responses were given as explanations for men's anger toward women. One man thought that men are angry because they are disappointed with their relationships which did not turn out the way the media painted them to be. Men are angry over being blamed and resented by women, thinks another. "Women spend too much money" and "women leave their stuff all over" were given as reasons, though the respondent wasn't sure if *anger* was the right word. Women don't express their feelings enough. Men are also mad over sexual harassment because they think it's carried way too far. One businessman offered the analogy of selling goods. If he wanted to sell something, he would put on a display that made the item look good and drew the attention of the customers. One would then be pleased if you succeeded in getting their attention. Women, he says, also want a man's attention, and they dress to make themselves look good. However, when they succeed in drawing the man's attention, they get mad.

One man felt very strongly that a main cause of anger is men's experience with divorce. He noted the increase in divorces in the last twenty years and the problem this has created for society, especially children. He thinks that a lot of the anger associated with divorces is passed on to the children. Referring to his own divorce, he said emphatically, "I don't think I've ever been in such a bitter battle in my life as I have going through a divorce. I didn't go into it angry, but it didn't take long to create it—a battle for life!" Over time, he became the aggressor because "she came after me with two lawyers and the gusto of a hound dog!" Her attitude was, "If I can't have you, nobody will," and set out to destroy him and make him suffer. After a three-year court battle, during which his children's loyalty was split, he got custody, settled down, and remarried. Though it ended well, he feels that the divorce took a toll on his children, his close friends, and him. With deep regret, he states that there are scars on his children that will never heal. He sees a lot of other men going through the same kind of situation. This man's story was particularly poignant because it seemed to him in retrospect that all this pain and suffering and expenditure of money and energy could have been avoided. As he looks back, it struck him that he married too young and too hastily. He went from high school to college to the navy and into marriage to the woman he dated in college. Soon after, he was juggling a new marriage, a job, and school (he went back to school after the navy). Then came the children. He felt as if he had missed out on a lot, got restless, and wanted out of the marriage. When he asked his wife for a divorce, she would not agree to it; they ended up going to a counselor but couldn't settle anything. Eventually she got to "a breaking point" and wanted a divorce and went after him "viciously." He remembers that there was a lot of pressure on his age group to get married right after high school and now feels that it is a good idea for people to wait and perhaps even to live together (though he morally abhors such a choice). But as he says philosophically, "There's nothing better than a good marriage, nothing in the world, and there's nothing worse than a bad marriage."

One man mused, "I don't see a lot of anger, but I'm not so sure that what I see is *not* anger. What I do see a lot is men that don't value women—at all; don't value them by any means, and that's just in men's circles sometimes that you have to travel in business." He goes on to say that a lot of men in business circles think that women are "nothing at all." He wonders if they inherited this attitude from their fathers.

Several men talked about the general state of affairs in our society and relations between women and men. A young husband and father was extremely disturbed about the resentment and anger between the sexes. He said he sees a lot of couples his age (thirties) where the woman works outside the home and no longer wants to do any housework. Her husband, who works too, ends up doing a fair amount of it. The problem is that nobody wants to be responsible for doing the work at home. Although men and women are "supposed to work together real well," he claims that it doesn't seem to happen much. "They're supposed to be partners," he says, "but seldom are; they are much more likely to be adversaries."

Another father and husband, in his fifties now and semiretired, was deeply troubled by how people are too busy and distracted (by television and commercialism) and bombarded by mixed messages about relationships. He thinks that men and women are becoming more and more confused, and yet we don't sit down with each other and discuss things. Men think that women don't understand them and won't talk to them or feel that the women don't want to talk to them. And women, instead of talking to the men, will go out with their girlfriends and bash the men. "Right now we just throw barbs at each other and only scratch the surface; we do not get to the core of the problem. We talk about superficial things." He strongly felt that we need to teach youngsters to deal with each other, approach problems constructively, and talk about feelings so that they don't end up where the adults are.

SUMMARY

Why Are Women Angry at Men?

This question can be answered by drawing on four different perspectives. One viewpoint is represented by the women's responses to what angers them about the men they know. These men anger them because they are irresponsible, domineering, insensitive, noncommunicative, condescending, and sexually abusive or obsessed. A second answer to why women are angry at men comes from the women's answers to what angers them about men in general. They are angry at men as a group because they are condescending, oversexed, physically and emotionally aggressive, and insensitive, treat them unfairly over work-related issues; and "they're men!" The third viewpoint is represented by women's answers to why other women are angry at men. Other women are angry because men are irresponsible, don't understand and support women, treat women unequally in the workplace, and have greater power and privilege. The final viewpoint on why women are angry at men comes from the men in the sample. They basically say that women are angry at men because of the lack of equality and men's lack of sensitivity and understanding.

All four sources of perception agree on lack of sensitivity and understanding as a major generator of anger. Issues related to lack of equality, especially in the workplace, comprise another source of anger, represented in three out of the four viewpoints (all except the men, they know). Thus, there is congruence on these two problems and both men and women seem to understand that these are sore points between them.

Lack of responsibility, on the other hand, is a theme of anger identified by women about men in their own lives and assumed to be a source of anger for other women; however, this was not mentioned at all by the men. Similarly, issues pertaining to sexual matters (overemphasis on sex, sexual exploitation) and physical aggression were important sources of anger for women but not identified by men. Thus, there is a big gap in perceptions in relation to these matters. It appears that men accurately perceive a couple of the problems that anger women but don't address most of them.

Why Are Men Angry at Women?

This question too can be answered using four viewpoints. Men themselves say that what angers them about women they know are a wide range of behaviors that they had no consensus on. No one behavior or attitude dominated. In regard to women in general, men say they are angered by women who are insensitive, irresponsible, and deceitful and manipulative. They believe other men are angry at women because of various consequences of the women's changing roles, as well as men's lack of understanding and support. The women in the sample believe that men are angry at women because of women's changing roles, which implies threats of one kind or another, as well as confusion.

Comparing the viewpoints shows that men perceive other men as getting angry for different reasons than they choose for themselves. Men cited a lot of personality attributes (deceitful, insensitive, rigid, talks too much, etc.) as sources of anger for the women in their lives. However, when judging why other men are angry at women, most of their responses focused on problems deriving from women's changing roles. They felt that other men were angry and frustrated because women are "stepping out of line," competing for men's jobs, challenging men's power and wisdom, and being less dependent on men. There was much more consistency between women's personal sources of anger and what they perceived to be other women's sources of anger.

There was congruence between women and men in regard to what angers men in general about women. Both sexes agree on the importance of women's changing roles as a source of anger for men in general. These perceptions tap into a shared understanding that gives men and women a foundation for solving this problem.

Answers on a personalized level by and large reflect different personal and interpersonal attributes (these people are seen as "acting like creeps"), while generalized perceptions reflect problems and changes in more structural terms (shifting roles, new opportunity structures, new sources of power). This is especially pronounced for men's anger at women, but the general pattern holds for women's anger at men.

Clearly, what was seen as angering other people was not necessarily perceived as a grievance on the personal level. For example, though various work-related inequalities figure prominently as explanations for anger between *other* women and men, this type of grievance was not a major cause of anger for women or men personally. When speaking about the men in their lives, relatively few women seemed concerned about men making more money, men not recognizing their contributions, or having less access to resources. A similar pattern occurred for men being angry at women. Men say that *other* men are really threatened by women who challenge men's power, take "men's jobs," earn their own income, and are stepping into new roles and attitudes. Yet men's personal explanations of what makes them angry do not reflect such concerns for the most part. This pattern did not hold for the issue of sensitivity and understanding. This area was seen as creating strong negative feelings for both themselves and others.

Implications

What do these findings imply about the accuracy of perceptions? Both sexes seem to be troubled by others who are not showing concern, understanding, and support. This bothers women about men and men about women, and each thinks the other sex is upset about this. Thus, there is no misperception, and this makes it more likely that steps can be taken to solve this problem, given the motivation to do so. Men and women also share views about the importance of changes in gender roles as a significant source of anger between the sexes. However, they tend to minimize the negative impact of these changes in their own lives. Women and men do not see eye to eye when it comes to irresponsible behavior. Such actions and attitudes are an important source of anger for women in their own lives, and they perceive other women as being angered by this as well. However, men do *not* see irresponsible behavior as a major source of concern for women (or for themselves), and thus this presents a major point of misperception.

These findings indicate that both women and men have a lot of work to do if their goal is to decrease anger between them. Men need to work on being more responsible; less domineering, condescending, and aggressive; more communicative; and promoting greater equality at home and in the workplace. Men need to rethink how they approach women sexually because women are frustrated by their overemphasis on sexual activities, sexual coercion, objectification, and, to a lesser extent, infidelity. Both men and women have to work on showing each other that they hear, support, respect, and care for each other. Both sexes need to stop acting as if they have a right to control each other, and both need to stop acting as if they are better than the other. Women need to address men's resentment over what are perceived to be manipulative, deceitful, and irresponsible actions. It is less clear what can be done about the changes accompanying women's roles. Most women are not going to be willing to vacate workplace premises. There is evidence that in some respects, workplace interactions between women and men are better than they were a while back; however, tensions over pay equity, career advancement, and sexual harassment may be increasing. It will take courage, sensitivity, perseverance, and perhaps a thicker skin on both men's and women's parts to traverse such tricky territory.

Chapter 7

Extent of Gender-Based Anger

Popular sources give the impression that women and men live in a perpetual state of anger. Undoubtedly, there are a considerable number of women and men who approach the other sex with resentment and distrust, and the number may be growing. Let's find out what a sample of seemingly well-adjusted, ordinary, mostly middle-aged and middle-class men and women have to say.

WOMEN AND PERSONALIZED ANGER

Female respondents were asked how often they get angry at men and women in general and at men and women they know personally. Responses ranged from "never" to "I think I've been mad at men all my life." In comparing both groups, it was clear that the men in their lives were more likely to be a source of anger than men in general. More than half said they "rarely" got angry at men in general, while less than one-fifth "rarely" got angry at men they know. For men in general, the extreme categories of "rarely" and "a lot" were mentioned most often, with very few answering "sometimes." For men they know, the number of responses increased as we move from "rarely," to "sometimes," to "a lot," with most responses falling into the "a lot" category.

When asked about how often they get angry at other women, both those they know and women in general, the same pattern held for both reference groups. The most common answer for both was "rarely," and the rest of the answers were scattered across "sometimes" and "a lot." Several women said they never got angry at either women they know or women in general.

Respondents were asked how angry men and other women were toward themselves. Close to two-thirds felt that men were not angry at them, and about one-third sensed some anger coming at them from men. Only two women said that they experience a lot of anger from men. One had a very angry husband who "comes in bitchin'." The other one talked about how a lot of men don't like strong women, and since she is a strong woman they get angry at her. Basically the same pattern occurred for anger and other women. The majority (slightly more than two-thirds) said that there was no anger from other women directed at them. About one-fifth felt that other women were sometimes angry at them, and only one said that other women were angry at her a lot. She saw these women as jealous of her single state, her looks, and her outgoing personality.

MEN AND PERSONALIZED ANGER

The men's answers were much more consistent and generally reflected lower levels of anger than the women's answers. Close to two-thirds of them said they "rarely" got angry at either women in general or at women they know. Very few admitted to getting angry "a lot" at either group of women. In fact, almost one-fifth of the males said they "never" got angry at women in general, and one never got angry at women he knows.

In reference to other men, their answers were spread out more evenly across the categories, although most of the men chose either "rarely" or "sometimes" as a response. One-fifth or less said "a lot" or "never" for both groups of men.

When men were asked about anger being directed at themselves, the majority (fifteen of twenty-five) sensed no anger from either women or other men. A significant minority (ten) of men felt "some" anger coming at them from both women and men. A couple of men indicated that they would experience more anger except that one "avoids certain kinds of people like the plague," and the other believes that most men would not let anyone know if they're angry; maybe one in a hundred would come right out and tell you they're mad at you. No man sensed "a lot" of anger directed at him. One man found this kind of question hard to answer. He claimed that he was not a "man's man"; he does not like to do "guy things" (he is artistic) and believes that he may be perceived as weak. He is not sure if these men avoid him because they are angry with him or uncomfortable with him.

Across both sets of respondents, "rarely" was chosen most often (it tied with "sometimes" for men talking about "men they knew") for all groups of people except when women talked about men they know. For this category "a lot" was chosen most often. Women also chose "a lot" more often in reference to men in general than anybody else. This implies that women get angry more often at men than men get angry at women.

This pattern is consistent with the position advocated by many feminists that women are more frustrated than men with current conditions. Women were less likely to get mad at other women in their lives than women in general. Although most said they rarely got angry at either group, more women chose "sometimes" and "a lot" for women in general. Men's responses indicated no real differences in frequencies (across categories) for either group of men. Overall, getting angry at anybody was a fairly infrequent event, with men being a particularly contented group.

WOMEN AND GENERALIZED ANGER

The picture for what I call generalized anger—anger perceived on behalf of other people toward a particular group—looks very different than for personalized anger. As you recall, most respondents indicated that they experienced anger *toward* others or *from* others infrequently. However, when asked how angry women in our society were at men, hardly any of the women thought this was a rare event. One woman did say that women are not angry at men, and another said she was not sure whether women are angry at men. A few had a hard time gauging the extent of anger and used men as a comparison group, saying that "more women are angry at men than vice versa." A handful thought it was somewhat of a problem, using phrases such as "a number of them are angry" or "a fair amount" are angry. However, the majority thought it is a common problem: there are a lot of angry women.

Common comments were, "A whole lot of women are angry at men"; "A lot of women are angry; it's widespread!" "This is an overall problem; there is a lot of anger." One articulate, professional woman said, "I think women are very angry with men. Generally, all women do is gripe about men and they are angry for all types of reasons!"

It was clear that for some women, their own feelings carried over into their assessment of other women's feelings. Said one, "More women are angry at men than vice versa. Men are so stupid! It's easy to get mad at them." Another exclaims, "We're very angry. A lot of anger is about the lack of equality. We hear about the laws and being treated equally, but that's a lot of lip-service. I don't believe it!" Another woman believed that more women are angry than men because women have "more concern with things going on in their lives."

Some of the side comments implied negative views of women. One young woman noted that a lot of women complain about men, but "when they see the men, they act like nothing is wrong." This same woman also made an interesting comment about how women decrease or dissolve their anger toward men. She said that a lot of women are angry, but "they get over it by complaining to other women—that's how they save their relationship with men." She also thought that a lot of women are angry at other women. One woman felt that women are separating themselves from men and in the process are looking for things to belittle about men. She commonly hears women saying things like "He can't do this without me" or "He just doesn't get it!" Although she understood these women's concerns and complaints, she didn't seem to approve of this treatment of men.

When women were asked about men's anger toward women, the pattern was generally the same but not as extreme. Again, the most common answer was that this is a problem of large proportions. Several women mentioned the large number of violent crimes against women as an indication of men's anger toward women. For example, one woman said that men "were very angry; that's why there is so much domestic violence." Several other explanations for widespread anger were mentioned, such as wives being more successful, men losing control in the workplace, men being frustrated over changing roles, and nasty divorces where the men "got screwed." But more women thought this was a minor problem than when they were talking about women's feelings toward men. For example, one woman said that she hardly ever sees men angry at women, that it's not a big problem. Another felt that it is currently not extensive but that it is a growing problem: "It's gonna get worse. It happens a lot more than the men admit to." One woman said sarcastically, "Most men are not angry at women. Why should they be? They don't have much to fear! Women are still taking care of the kids and doing the housework."

A few women said they were not sure of the extent of men's anger toward women, although one felt that it was probably escalating and another said she didn't see it in her own social circles but wondered about domestic abuse and violence and its relationship to anger. Another woman in this group said that it's hard to give an overall estimate of angry men because it depends on where you look. She is very active in church and sees no angry men there, but in her country neighborhood, there are many extremely angry men. She recounted stories of husbands who go after their wives with guns. When she was asked for referrals, she said she couldn't give me the names of these men because she literally feared for my safety or feared that talking about their anger would stir them up so that their family members would suffer the repercussions.

Several women mentioned that there were a lot of angry men but that the source of the anger was not gender related. One woman talked about a "major" group of men who believe you have to have power over others and these men act in an aggressive fashion. These men, she says, may not be angry at women but at themselves because they don't know how to get power and then they get angry and let it out on a woman. Another woman thinks that there is anger directed at women but she doesn't think the men are angry with the women themselves. She likens it to child abuse where people may not be angry at the child but at their circumstances. She thinks that men don't realize this; a woman is a good target, a good punching bag. She sees a problem with men directing anger at women, but the women are not the source of the problem. Another woman mused that men are angry at other men and at their life situation, and they take this anger out on women.

MEN AND GENERALIZED ANGER

When men were asked for their assessment of how angry other men are at women, the answers ranged from "no anger," "I'm not sure," "not much anger," or "a fair amount of anger," to "a lot of anger," with the number of responses increasing in a geometric fashion. Only one man said he perceived no general anger aimed at women. A couple were not sure of the extent of anger today. One thought that there was more anger in the 1960s, 1970s, and 1980s. Just a few men thought there was some but not much anger. One felt that a small proportion of men are angry at particular women and that this is a consistent problem. Several others mentioned that relatively small numbers of men (10 to 20 percent) are angry and that these tend to be uneducated, lower-class men. One man cryptically said, "I don't see a lot of anger, but I'm not so sure that what I see is *not* anger"; however, he does see "a lot of men who don't value women." About one-fourth of the sample saw a "fair amount" of anger directed at women. One reasoned that there must be some angry men because of the rapes perpetrated on women. He also has a brother-in-law who "lives in anger" at his wife.

The most common response was that there is a lot of anger from a lot of men. One man claims, "About 60 to 70 percent of the men are angry if they were honest and you really talked about it." He says he sees a lot more anger than he used to. Several men used the high rate of crime against women and divorce as indicators of high anger levels. One man said, "It must be pretty bad if the divorce rate is so high. Both sexes must be mad at each other." Another states, "Given the assault on women, there is a problem." "Men are very angry," says another. "A lot of it is associated with divorce." One man explained that a lot of men are angry (he guessed 70 to 75 percent), but he thought they were probably angry with life in general and women simply become a convenient target. He also felt that most of these men don't realize that they are angry about other things.

When it came to the men's perceptions of women's anger toward men, a different pattern emerged. Many were more unsure about women's anger than about men's anger. Roughly equal numbers of men felt that there was a little anger and a lot of anger, and the most common response was that there was a fair amount of anger. When asked how angry women are at men today, one man said, "I don't see that really. The women I see seem content." Another felt that only a small proportion of women are angry but that most women are confused. He says, "Most women aren't really angry, but they're horribly confused. They don't know how they fit in with men, where they want to go, what the ideal woman is, is it okay to get old?"

The typical answer (given by one-third of the men) was that there is a fair amount of anger on the part of the women. Several said that more women are angry than men, and they judged less than 25 percent of the men to be angry. One-fifth of the men thought that a lot of women are angry. This is about half the number of men who judged men to be angry at those levels. One man exclaimed, "Oh, very angry! The more progress they've made, the angrier they are because it didn't come a long, long time ago."

In comparison, when women are asked to judge others' state of anger, the most common response is that they see a lot of angry women and men. When men are asked, however, they see more men being angry at women than women being angry at men. Men are also more likely to admit that they don't know and don't understand what is going on with women today. This kind of reaction was highly unusual for the women that were interviewed.

There is a discrepancy between what men say about their own personal levels of anger toward women (which are relatively low) and what they perceive to be true for other men, whom they see getting angry a lot at women. Women are more consistent in that they admit to getting angry a lot at men themselves, and they see a lot of other women being angry at men as well. This could mean that women have a harder time separating personal feelings from others' feelings. It could be that men can't admit their own anger but project it to other men.

From listening to these men and women it became clear that women are the angrier sex, or at least they expressed anger more openly and forcefully than the men did. Both verbally and nonverbally, the women communicated a much greater intensity of anger than the men. Quite a few men, in fact, said they weren't really "angry" at women but irritated or annoyed by them and that women generally treated them really well. Very few women stated such sentiments. Also, when women and men were asked how often they get angry, only women's responses could be categorized as "a lot."

Chapter 8

On the Edge of Ambivalence

In order to situate the anger feelings in a larger, social context, each person was asked to share his or her thoughts (positive and negative) on the changes that have occurred in our society regarding expectations and behaviors associated with being women and men. Which ones do they like? Which ones are they troubled by? It turned out that overall, there was a remarkable similarity of viewpoints: both women and men overwhelmingly said they had mixed feelings about the changes. Twenty of the women and twenty-one of the men saw both good and bad results of the changes. Only one man and one woman had nothing good to say about the changes, and three and four, respectively, were happy with what has been happening in our society in regard to changing roles of men and women.

WOMEN—ON THE POSITIVE SIDE OF AMBIVALENCE

Two changes stood out above all others in terms of what women like about gender-related changes in our society today. One was the fact that women are perceived to have greater opportunities and choices than in the past. Although most of the women referred to greater choices for women, some mentioned that they were glad that men have more choices as well. The other change mentioned most often in a favorable light was the greater equality women today enjoy. Some of the women who talked about liking the emerging equality and increasing opportunities followed up their statements with disclaimors such as, "but I'm not a feminist!" or "I'm not a women's libber. I like being treated like a woman!" This sentiment is consistent with the negative image of feminists in the larger society. Some women were eager to accelerate changes along these dimensions. One woman said she "welcomed the changes, but things should change more." She would like to see a woman president. One the other hand, this woman does not see women in all jobs. Although she really likes it that women can work and be what they want to be, she cautions that some jobs are better done by a man, such as construction work. A young, white professional woman feels that women can do what they want today but men do not have this same freedom. For example, they can't be househusbands without ridicule; she can wear dresses or pants, paint her lips or not, work outside the home or not, and still be considered a "good" and "normal" woman.

Greater power and more independence were also mentioned as things that were liked today. "The changes give women more of a say-so," says one woman. "Women and men should not be doormats!" Another likes it "that women are now in powerful leadership positions." Still another applauds the fact "that women are less likely to be second-class citizens and have the freedom to go places." A young, vivacious black woman says, "I like where it's going in the sense that I see women becoming more independent, but it may be that women have become too independent." She recounted a story of telling her mother that she didn't need a man, that she could get artificially inseminated if she wanted children, and her "mom about died." Despite such thoughts of independence, she wonders if people haven't become too self-centered and not tied enough to other family members. Generally the women expressed their support for women running their own households, earning their own income, managing money, and making decisions and that "a woman can provide for herself with or without a man."

Relatively few women mentioned changes that included men. Most of them focused on changes that would benefit women as a group. However, some liked the changes because they have brought things like greater involvement of men around the house. They see more fathers who are actively involved with their children by taking them to doctors' appointments and helping out with carpooling. Also mentioned was that more men are helping with chores around the house. An employed mother of two grins and says, "I love seeing my husband fold a load of clothes." A couple of women praised the changes for getting men and women talking to each other more and that as a result men and women are working together more as a family.

Several women were glad that we are less likely to stereotype individuals today, that "we are trying to treat men and women as human beings rather than stereotypes." Another also likes the decrease in stereotyping and greater openness and that we are less limited by roles. However, she feels there is still a lot of such limitation. Another woman who cited more openness as a benefit said, "Rather than as stereotypes, people can finally begin to act out of their gifts and their talents." Finally, one woman was appreciating the fact that as a result of the women's movement, there is more help available for those who need shelters or counseling.

MEN—ON THE POSITIVE SIDE OF AMBIVALENCE

Just like the women, the overwhelming majority of the men had mixed or ambivalent feelings about the gender-related changes in our society. Only a few said they liked all the changes, and only one said he liked none of the changes.

The men were most appreciative of the move toward greater equality between women and men.   When talking about equality, most of the men mentioned their support for equal pay for equal work. This principle clearly is widely endorsed by both the women and the men in this sample, as it is in the population at large. A young man who works for a church organization talked about how the idea of fair and equal wages is supported in the Scriptures. The Old Testament describes an industrious woman who is in real estate, and people are urged to give her "her due" and to honor her. One young man unequivocally welcomed the changes and said, "Probably what makes me the happiest is the fact that women are now treated equally to men in all respects." Although no one else felt that women had yet achieved equality "in all respects," many men saw our society heading in this direction and were happy about it.

Another change that was mentioned fairly frequently was flexibility in roles. One middle-aged white professional man liked the open roles and has taken advantage of them in his own life. He participated actively as a father with his two children. He enjoyed being able to give them their bath and put them to bed. Another man who liked the role flexibility said that he and his wife have an "almost strange relationship." Both work; he does most of the cooking (because he likes to cook), and they share cleaning of the house. He smiles and says that it works for them. He believes that his wife "wasn't made to cook, clean, etc." and that he can't change her. As he puts it, "You have to deal with what you got!" He is not sure this kind of arrangement is for everyone else. Others shared a concern about how these arrangements could be worked out but agreed that "as long as people can work it out between themselves," they are all for it. One man who likes flexible roles qualifies his feelings by saying that when children are involved, the flexibility must be sacrificed and the mother (preferably) should stay at home.

A man in his early forties who is married but childless describes how he and his wife have almost reversed traditional roles. She is the primary breadwinner, and she controls the finances and a lot of the decision making. He readily admits that she works harder and longer hours and does more mental work than he does. He typically works at temporary jobs that tend to require a lot of physical labor. He also takes care of the house and does the cooking since his work schedule is much more flexible and less consistent than hers.

Several men liked the changes because they have forced men to change their own behaviors and attitudes. Said one, "The changes have opened up our eyes to search for ourselves how to do things." Another mentioned that "men are held in check more, held more accountable for their actions." In a similar vein, a man in the health professions said that because of the changes, men operate on a different plane with their staff. He seemed ambivalent about that; on the one hand, it decreased the likelihood of misunderstandings and problems like sexual harassment, but on the other hand, it required extra effort. A man in his fifties who has been divorced and now works part-time likes the changes but that's because he "has an agenda." He believes that his freedom is inextricably intertwined with women's: "I'm not any freer than you are. It's gonna end up doing a whole lot for men, so I'm all for it. I think it's wonderful!"

The new perspectives and challenges brought by the changes were mentioned by several men as the things they really like about the direction our society is heading in. He's glad to see women in the professional arena, said one man. He thinks they add a balance and a new perspective. In fact, in some professions, like dentistry, for example, a woman might be preferred by some clients. A woman might be better at dentistry when dealing with children since they probably see her as less threatening. When questioned what he meant by "a new perspective," his answer was that women tend to be less aggressive, less competitive, and less action oriented; they are good at acknowledging and recognizing issues; and they bring "a softness" to the workplace. One man who is semiretired from a medical profession says without hesitation that the best employees and colleagues he has had in the past twenty years have been women. They have met his needs and the clients' needs better than men. They have "brought a whole new perspective to everything; they are essential."

Some men appreciate the fact that today there is more sharing between women and men. One likes "sharing the tasks of life." He believes that this allows for greater communication between men and women and ultimately makes for a "more integrative relationship." Another man stressed the benefit of greater understanding between the sexes that can come from working and sharing responsibilities. Some respondents were glad that women finally are getting more recognition for their talents and abilities. A man in his sixties thinks that women have a tremendous advantage emotionally and that this is finally beginning to be understood. He thinks that women might be better than men at surgery, lab work, or scientific endeavors generally because they are better at doing work requiring precision. Men also expressed satisfaction over the fact that there are generally more opportunities for women today. One man pointed out that he still has trouble visualizing a woman as president but nevertheless hopes to see one in this office. He explains that he sees women as more emotional or at least as showing emotions more so than men, and this makes it hard for him to see women as presidents or soldiers. He added that he doesn't doubt women's competence as soldiers because he knows "they'll kill you if they're mad at you." He has no hesitation in going to a physician who is female; in fact, he may even prefer it. Men added two final comments to the list of things they like. One felt that the changes allow us as a society to use many more resources. The other mentioned women's increased assertiveness as something that he found "refreshing" though sometimes disconcerting.

Some men indicated that their views were not always so positive. A man who now is "very happy with the changes" confided that he was not always that way. When women entered his profession, he "had a rough time at first." He felt that these women came in and "overdid it" in the process of proving their competence. Several men expressed unbridled enthusiasm and a high level of endorsement for the changes in our society. One man stated, "I'm fine with 95 percent of everything!"

WOMEN—ON THE NEGATIVE SIDE OF AMBIVALENCE

Though most women felt good about some of the societal trends and changes, almost all of them simultaneously were anxious, troubled, and sometimes angry about a host of issues and problems spawned by the gender-related changes in the past thirty years or so. At the top of their list of concerns and dislikes was what I will call the blurring of gender roles.

Sitting in her sunny kitchen, I listened to a young, articulate, and very concerned woman share her thoughts about what she called the "muddying of male and female roles":

We've got to realize there is a difference, more than just the plumbing. My emotional makeup is different from my husband's. I mother better. I know that some men do a very good job; my husband does, but my children still come to me. It's not bad to have separate roles as long there is respect and love. We are trying to do away with roles. We need equality, but we need to realize there's a difference.

This sentiment was echoed more times than any other. Another woman said she would like to see some differences remain. Women *should* be softer and be proud of being female. Although she thinks it's all right for men to be nurturing and that we can encourage it in men, this kind of behavior should come from the woman. She believes that the sexes are different for good reason. She used the analogy of persons from a different country or culture. These people have their own culture and we can never make them like us or us like them, but we do need to find some way to get along, especially where anger is concerned.

Some feel that we have "stepped too far in some areas." Although they generally approve of increased opportunities and power for women, they should not go in all places. For example, says one respondent, women should not go to the Citadel. If she wants to go to a military school, let her go to an all-female military school. Girls should go to *Girl* Scouts, not *Boy* Scouts! A middle-aged mother of two said that she "is leery of change; it has some danger in it." She went on to elaborate that typically when people move out of the space they have been in, there is a tendency to move too far out on an extreme. Thus, women may go too far into realms that they were never intended to go by God, she says. She has no problem with women going to work out of the home, but she is afraid that the proper balance in a husband-wife relationship will be upset by women who are too aggressive. She sees women as going too far and predicts they "will hit the wall before they bounce back." According to her beliefs, the husband is the leader in the home and the wife needs to accept that. She stressed that a man's leadership does not imply dominance: "No Christian man would lord it over a woman or put a woman down." Using a personal example in her own marriage where she and her husband disagreed over the children's schooling, she says she found strength in the fact that she was submitting to his leadership and going along with his preference. She also pointed out that when she could no longer do what he asked of her, he accepted that and even apologized for having asked her to go against her own doubts.

Another major concern voiced by this group of women was the feeling that as a society we have lost our moral bearings and lost sight of important things like the family, sacrifice, and commitment. One woman talked at length about such issues:

It bothers me in all these changes that we seem to have lost the family unit. We're working so hard to make men and women equal, we've lost the family. That's why we see a lot of our problems today, because men are growing up without women who've ever loved them; they don't have that mother because she's not there or because the father left and the mother spends all her time trying to make ends meet.

This woman also feels that we have lost the church and our morals as to what is right and wrong. She laments that "nothing is wrong anymore," that there is "a lot of chaos in our society." In her opinion, these changes have put men and women at odds with each other, which was never intended to be that way. "We're meant to complement each other and work together; when you take away the family and [men and women] don't work together, then there is a lot of anger."

Another woman says the changes have been positive but that they have created serious repercussions and social distress. She thinks that men are "very much threatened by women advancing up through the ranks professionally and economically." They are uncomfortable when the wife makes more money because it "lessens their manhood and diminishes their testosterone flow." Despite these kinds of problems, she thinks that we need to keep striving for these changes. A woman upset about the morals of the country said, "They have gone to hell." She feels there is no commitment on the part of men and women today. This exact sentiment was expressed by another woman who is sorry that people don't put the same amount of energy into marriage as they used to. This creates a lot of problems. She mentioned that she had talked to a judge who claimed that 90 percent of juveniles he sees in court come from a home without a father. She sees women's increased independence as a double-edged sword. Although she values this independence in herself and others and her own mother encouraged her to get a job so she could support herself, she thinks this independence leads to more divorces. Ironically, she and her husband were previously married, and she admits readily that she did not put as much effort into her first marriage as she could have or as she is putting into her second marriage.

On a somewhat less serious note, a thirty-eight-year-old unmarried mother of three says regretfully, "I'm an old-timey girl I like a man opening doors for me. We need to teach people to be polite. Today, boys are not taught to respect a girl or even help a girl in trouble."

Many other issues were raised as the women discussed what bothered them about the recent gender-related changes. Most of these were mentioned by only one, two, or three individuals. Several women complained about women who are too pushy or militant in trying to force change on people. As one put it, "I don't like the women's lib thing—women who put themselves above men and belittling them." In a similar vein, one married mother of three denounced militant women who, in trying to be like men, are making men so insecure that they don't know what to do.

Some complained of too little time and of life being too hectic, chaotic, and confusing. One middle-aged homemaker and mother of two said wistfully, "Life was so simple one hundred years ago. Each sex knew what to do. Now it's too easy for men to hire someone to do yardwork and play video games themselves." She feels that there is confusion about men's and women's work today. She does not advocate separate roles again but thought it was easier the old way. Another middle-aged mother of one who owns and operates her own small business is unhappy about feeling overworked. "When both have a career, it can cause a lot of chaos," she says. "There's not enough time, and this can build up anger." "We don't have enough time to take care of each other; there are too many demands on us," states a harried professional woman and mother of two. She said the worst thing about being a woman today was having "too many hats to wear." "I hate it!" she said with great frustration.

The fact that so many mothers choose to work outside the home or feel that they have to work outside the home bothered several women. One recalls how her own mother was always there for her and her brother while she was growing up. Today, she sees too many mothers who put their children in day care, and she fears that the children do not get proper attention. Having to work outside the home and doing a "second shift" inside the home was also mentioned as a strong dislike. Several women were against the lowering of standards in the workplace or having different standards for women and men. One said she "was unhappy about giving people jobs even if they're not qualified." Other issues mentioned were "women not getting enough recognition for what they do," "the idea of homosexuals raising children (though it is not my job to judge them but God's job)," and not getting the "training" we need on how to make things work and subsequently "floundering around." The last statement was made by a woman who likes the changes but sees a myriad of family system problems stemming from them. She believes that men and women are still being raised in a traditional fashion (though her own mother and father had an unconventional arrangement), but meanwhile our values and goals have changed. Somehow we need to learn how to live according to these new ideals. One woman had a suggestion along these lines. She recommended that instead of having a "take your daughter to work" day, we need a "take your son to work" day because it is the boys who need to learn to value women and what they do.

The one woman who didn't like any of the changes wants to go back to more traditional days. She "really dislikes women going off to war, flying bomber planes, driving tanks, etc." According to her, "Men should not sit at home and be the housekeeper, feed the baby, or wash dishes." These are not men's jobs but women's jobs, and if a woman lets him do it, there is something wrong with her. This holds even if she is working full time; it is still her job, though "he can keep her company." What is interesting is that this young woman grew up in a home where her father, whom she says she adores and idolizes, was nontraditional and did all of the "women's work" after he and his wife divorced. In fact, he had custody of the two children.

MEN—ON THE NEGATIVE SIDE OF AMBIVALENCE

An interesting and unexpected finding was that the biggest concern voiced by the men involved the welfare of children. Although many men had singled out flexible and more open roles as one of the things they really like, this change is also a source of problems because it has left so many children unattended or with significantly less attention. As one put it, "Couples will try to work and try to raise a family at the same time, and it's the children who are the ones that are going to suffer from it." Another is bothered that some women *have* to work so much and that there are other women who *choose* to leave the home and their children when their husbands make plenty of money. One man recalls that some of the trouble he got into as a child was because no adult was around. He sees too many children spending too much time without an adult around. A young father of three laments the way parents relate to children. If there are children, the wife should stay at home, he believes, because the woman is typically a better nurturer. He told of his own wife who had a job she loved but gave it up in order to stay home with their children. He admits to being jealous of the time she has with the children and says he sacrifices his own career to an extent in order to spend more time with his children. He is afraid that a lot of people don't understand this whole issue well. Another man, now in his fifties, a father of three children who are now grown, feels that "the whole thing can go too far. You can't have too many people leaving the home if children are there." He is not sure whether children are better off with a mother or father staying home, but it is best when both have input rather than just one.

Nationwide surveys on changing attitudes about working and mothering document a strong long-term trend toward increasing approval of women working outside the home while raising children. In 1972 one-third of Americans still disapproved of working women whose husbands were capable of supporting them; this dropped to 20 percent in 1994 (Farley 1996). The responses of at least the men in my sample indicate that some of these attitudes may be reversing themselves.

Some talked about children in a slightly different, though related context. One says he is worried about children today because they seem a lot more spoiled and indulged. He has an employed friend who complains constantly about all the work she has to do, and yet she has two daughters, age eleven and fourteen, who are rarely asked to help out. She won't ask them to do work around the house. Though he did not say it directly, it could be that this mother feels guilty about being gone a lot and one way of assuaging her guilt is by spoiling them. An elderly man who is now retired spoke at length about today's children:

I think young people nowadays have a tough time. I wouldn't want to be a youngster anymore. I think there are just too many—I don't know what's the word I'm looking for—

young people are faced with too many temptations now, both men and women. You've got your drugs; we may have had them way, way back too, but it was not to the extent that it is now. You've got much more open sex now than you ever had before much more teen pregnancy and so forth. You may have had some back then, but back then it was more hushed up. And all the diseases you have now. I think the temptations now… I think it takes a strong person to get through that.

He wonders how all this will affect them when they are in their twenties and thirties in their relationships with spouses and their own children. He grants that it may make them stronger, but he worries nevertheless.

The next most commonly mentioned problem was women in the military. Although some thought that women can handle the rigors involved, it was thought to be a bad idea because it causes too many problems between the women and men who live and serve together. They ought not to be on the same ships and in the same schools. The problems arise either because men can't handle women in the military emotionally because men are too aggressive, or because when women and men are in such close quarters, there is bound to be sexual attraction and this will result in competition, jealousy, and a loss of effectiveness. One man talked at length about rape in the military. He was incensed at the way the government handled it. The government should have expected it, he says; they cannot stop it by law, and the way they write the laws makes no sense to him. According to him, the laws make it so that either women have to accuse the men of rape or be guilty themselves of violating regulations. "Common sense should prevail more than it does," he huffs. Some thought that women simply "were not made for that" or that they could fight but should never be in a position to be prisoners of war or that it was okay for women to be in the military but they should go to all-female schools. No one liked the idea of women in combat.

Some of the most fervent statements were made in regard to perceived government interference. These men had strong opinions about affirmative action, quotas, eliminating all-male schools, and related efforts aimed at making things more equal between women and men. One man says pointedly, "I'm all for women being successful—*if* they earn it." He is totally against changing rules, regulations, and standards in order for women to pass. "If she wants to compete in a man's world, then let her live in those conditions." That these feelings are widely shared is evident by a recent announcement of the army in regard to fitness standards (*Washington Post* 1997). Citing "overwhelming evidence of divisions between the men and women in its ranks," the army is going to narrow the differences in standards for the semiannual fitness test. The currently lower requirements for sit-ups and push-ups by women are seen as a "serious problem" for the men. Brigadier General Evelyn Foote was quoted as saying that "men cannot accept the fact that because of gender there should be different standards." Survey results showed that only half of the male troops felt that women pull their load in comparison to almost all the male and female soldiers feeling that men pull their load. Other survey results indicated a real gender gap in attitudes about women having an advantage over men when it comes to having a successful military career and about female soldiers getting treated better than male soldiers; in both cases more men believed this to be true than female soldiers. Interestingly enough, there was less of a gap when they were asked if women should be allowed to do any job "for which they can qualify." Almost 70 percent of the men and 80 percent of the women agreed. So it isn't that men don't believe that women can or should do this type of work, but that they should have to do the same work as the men.

Another man objected to he idea that you can't have an all-male college. He claims that sometimes we do things for shock value and not for general social advancement and that is what we are doing in reference to this issue. He said that the men at the Citadel went there under a specific set of assumptions and that it's unfair to change them: "Integration for the sake of integration doesn't serve a purpose." He argues that if the Citadel was the *only* place where women can get military training, then it would be okay to let women enter. But why not have them go to an all-female military school? He believes that these may benefit women more than co-ed schools.

Another complaint about the current social scene involved the idea of getting rid of differences between the sexes. A white middle-aged professional says what bothers him is "the tacky way women's lib has tried to force change down people's throats." A few seconds later he added that maybe they had to. "Let men be men and women be women!" says a middle-aged married man. A retired man is upset by how feminists want everything to be equal. He thinks there are basic differences between the sexes in strength and nurturance, and these should be respected. Another retired man dislikes the feminist movement for wanting to say that women are better off without men and that men are holding women down. "This is bad," he says. "We have to realize there's a big difference in women and men. We should capitalize on this, not argue about it, not act superior. This makes us a good match! Why say, Hah, I'm better at this than you! Neither is better!"

A few other problems were mentioned by more than one man: women's unwillingness to submit themselves to their husbands, the growing acceptance of homosexuality, and the declining importance of the family. One man said, "The perfect scenario is: man who submits to God, she submits to man." He stressed the need for "spiritual unity" where the man has the vision and the woman makes him stick to it or keeps the vision going. He claims that without women's persistence, men would "fall on their faces." A woman *can* have her own vision, he says, but usually she submits to a man. A young man who works in a religious setting stressed that God sees women as just as capable as men, but gave men the leadership role in marriage. "But you must remember," he adds, "that the husband should serve the wife." He provided an analogy of a governor's relationship to his or her state. We need a governor for a state, but his or her purpose is not to dominate but to serve the people of the state and do what is best for them. Similarly, a husband should be willing to lay down his life or a job for his wife. It is clear that these views were expressed by a group of men who have a strong relationship with their church and God.

A couple of men, both young, one religious and one not, were troubled by homosexuality. One man says that although he likes a lot of the changes, he doesn't like it that these changes have opened some doors, such as a greater acceptance of homosexuality. A slightly older man said he is not sure about "all the hype about homosexuality." He increasingly hears people talking about the idea that it is "cool to be gay," and he worries that this will encourage the behavior too much. A few of the men were genuinely concerned about the breakdown of the family as a result of women in the workplace as well as other factors. A couple of men lamented that things don't revolve around the family as much as they used to and that today there is too much focus on making money as a way of finding happiness. They wonder whether it really takes two incomes or whether we simply want too many material goods.

A couple of men, one young and one in his fifties, expressed a lot of concern about the confusion over roles today. The middle-aged man felt that men have a poorer idea of what is expected of them today and have a harder time dealing with the changes. Roles are no longer "cut and dried," and it is the males who seem more insecure and confused. He believes that it is imperative for people to discuss these issues and teach youngsters how to deal with each other. Another man sees a lot of males and females who feel unfairly treated and take injustice personally. The result is a lot of anger. A lot of couples his age (thirties) don't want to take responsibility for doing the work that needs to be done at home. The woman, who typically works outside the home, no longer wants to do housework, and this forces the man to do some. Instead of working together as partners, he thinks they are more likely to be adversaries. Another man commented that men today are insecure and have a hard time handling assertive women. "It's making men change!" he concludes.

A few miscellaneous comments were made on top of all those listed above. One man was upset that many women still see women in negative ways. Another doesn't like dealing with women who think they have been mistreated; he says he is not even sure what "equality" means. Women are too assertive for another man. Finally, a middle-aged man who has cut back on his work is troubled over how busy we are today. "It's like a beehive hum," he exclaims. "It's like we're on a blasting pad" and there is always more coming at us. We are way too distracted by television and commercialism and are getting mixed messages. We tend to talk about superficial things; we "just throw barbs at each other and only scratch the surface." We need to get at the core of the problem and talk about our feelings, both positive and negative.

CONCLUSION

It was interesting to find that the men and women were so similar in their overall assessment of the gender-related changes of the past few decades. The great majority of them had mixed feelings, in that they saw a lot of things they liked but were troubled by some aspects of change. Very few were unequivocally for or against the changes. To some extent, these findings are similar to those of Anthony Astrachan (1986) who interviewed men across the country. He sorted the men into four groups based on their feelings toward women's rights. There were the "opponents," who were explicitly against equality, believing it would be destructive of society. They used biology and the Bible as sources for their convictions. In my sample, there were only one man and one woman who were true "opponents," and only one of these spoke of God's plan for the sexes. The other didn't seem to know why she was so vehemently against the changes. Other individuals referred to their religious beliefs in discussing their answers and were obviously strongly influenced by these, but these beliefs did not result in categorical denial of the goal of equality. Almost all of them endorsed equal rights, although they thought these rights should not extend into every area of life. While they had no problem with women working outside the home and even assuming leadership positions, they insisted on the man being the leader (although a benign, loving, and fair one) in the household. They thought that women should be allowed to pursue any occupational interest, with the exception of combat roles or when they had small children at home.

Astrachan labeled those who intellectually approved of equality but who couldn't live up to it "ambivalents." These men (he interviewed only men) accept women's competence in traditionally masculine jobs but have trouble living and working with them. He figures that this was the most common type. Some of the men in my sample seemed to border on this type, though they seemed reluctant to state such views outright. One man in a male-dominated profession talked about how he had initially resented the women coming into the field because they acted inappropriately, but concluded that he had no problems with them today. However, women and men mentioned fairly frequently how *other* men and women had problems with women (and men) who pursued feminist goals.

Astrachan's "pragmatists" commonly say that they are not for women's liberation but then cite views compatible with the women's movement. Some of these cropped up in my interviews, though women were more likely to disown the "feminist" or "women's lib" title than the men.

The last group Astrachan identified was the "supporters," who were openly in favor of women's rights and tried to live their life consistent with these goals. He estimates this group as being very small—around 5 to 10 percent of his sample. I would say that this type of person was very common in my sample among both the males and females.

Although almost all of these individuals expressed serious concerns about recent changes, almost none seemed to feel that changes in roles (especially women's) have been an affront to them personally and that they feel victimized and hostile as a result. Again, I was looking for ordinary, not angry, people to interview, and therefore this is not surprising. Many of these individuals, however, saw lots of anger and strong anger, even aggression, on the part of generalized others, both male and female.

It was interesting that it was the men who answered this question with more conviction and vehemence than the women. A lot of the men felt very strongly about issues such as affirmative action and women in the military, and it was at this point in the interview that they seemed most agitated. Several men were extremely upset with the government, which they saw as meddling in unproductive ways. In contrast, the female respondents tended to get most agitated when talking about how men (especially husbands and fathers) had treated them in their relationships.

In the introduction to *Bridging Separate Gender Worlds* (1997) Carol Philpot and her co-authors state that "In the last 30 years in the U.S. women have begun to define themselves differently and the impact of this redefinition on men, women, and couples' relationships has been revolutionary indeed." The feelings and thoughts shared by the men and women in this sample testify how not only women but men as well are redefining what each can and should do in their dealings with each other and children. Many are not willing to throw out some of the traditional expectations, but they are clearly choosing new goals—equality, role sharing, and emotional intimacy. However, they are not sure whether they are following the right path to reach these goals.

Chapter 9

Toward Gender Peace

An act of justice closes the book on a misdeed; an act of vengeance writes one of its own. (Marilyn vos Savant 1996)

The overarching goal for this book and research is to improve relations between men and women in a context of equality. It was not until around the middle of the twentieth century that we seriously began talking about gender equality—at home, at work, at play. This conversation has increasingly become heated as each party seeks to maintain or gain a more favorable and just position. It is clear from talking to this group of men and women that they are troubled by many things about each other as well as their own sex and the direction in which society at large is moving. It is also clear that many of the respondents are learning valuable lessons along the way. They are finding better ways to live with their significant others, and many are working on changing what they perceive as unproductive, unhealthy modes of anger expression. Before summarizing some of the important learnings, let the respondents share their thoughts on how to deal with anger ideally and what can be done to improve relationships between the sexes.

IDEAL WAYS OF EXPRESSING ANGER: "BE ANGRY BUT SIN NOT!"

Although there was much variation among the people I interviewed in regard to how they handled their own and others' anger, how often they got angry, and why they got angry, there was great consensus between both the women and men on how to express anger ideally. In fact, the answers were so repetitive that I did not ask every person about this. However, I asked most of the respondents, and the results were quite predictable, with few exceptions.

The essence of their advice was to calm down, sit down, and rationally discuss what angered you. Except for the person who said you shouldn't have gotten angry in the first place and thus there is no need to discuss it, there was unanimity on the importance of expressing rather than hiding feelings of anger. In response to the question, "How should we express anger ideally?" a young woman said with frustration and conviction, "I don't know, but I just know it needs to be expressed! A lot of people are sick—physically and emotionally—because they did not know how to handle anger." She suggested that if people could not go to the other person directly, they might need to write a letter or talk into a recorder if that's what it takes. Most people also felt that the anger should be expressed immediately or soon after the anger episode because otherwise, the anger "festers" and grows even worse. Most stressed how crucial it is to "stay in control." One man urges us not to deal with things "in the heat of the moment" because this "compounds things exponentially." He advises, "First get control of yourself, and then address it in a matter-of-fact, straightforward way. Lay the cards on the table, deal with it, and get on with it. The problem tends to be that one party or the other holds back some cards and plays them at a later time. If you don't know what you're dealing with, you can't deal with it."

The majority felt that when you talk to the people involved, it should be in a calm, quiet, rational manner. However, some disagreed. One woman says, "It's all right to yell things out—it has never hurt us." Another says that anger could be expressed in different ways, and "It could be that yelling is your particular style." One man feels that people don't have to be calm: "Sometimes screaming is what is needed for a release. Some of my friends like the sound of broken glass." Indeed, it could be that being perfectly calm may not get the message across; some people will believe that someone is angry only if he or she yells.

A few people suggested specific techniques for the discussion of anger. One man said, "Ideally, people should do a version of hand holding." He had heard somewhere that if you're angry at your wife, you should hold her hand and tell her what's going on because it's very difficult to have a fight while holding hands. Another man felt that one should discuss differences in the presence of a mediator. A middle-aged woman advises not to attack or lash out at the other person. You need to say what bothers you, but you can do it without cutting the other person down. This woman used to be angry all the time and attack her spouse but has recently changed her ways and says with great relief, "You can't imagine how it feels not to be a time bomb!"

In answering this question, a lot of people laughed in a way that indicated that they didn't believe that their suggestions would or could be lived up to. Their answers to earlier questions, indeed, corroborate this view. However, it is also clear that many people in this sample are working toward their ideals. With one exception, all respondents saw anger as natural, inevitable, and even useful; however, they respected its power to hurt and destroy and thus stressed the importance of guarding our tongues and actions.

OTHER THOUGHTS ON ANGER

Each person was also asked for any other thoughts on anger—any other suggestions, learnings, or warnings—they wanted to pass on to those who read this book. Most of the respondents did. Quite a few women and men reiterated the importance of not losing control when angry because of the destructive power of anger. This had been mentioned over and over again when discussing ideal anger expression. One woman is truly upset about the way she says "mean, hateful things" when she's angry because she blurts things out without thinking. This really bothers her, and she advises people to step back, count to ten, take a walk, or do whatever else it takes to be able to think rationally again. Another person simply said, "Get control of your anger. It doesn't lead anywhere good." A young black male believes that anger can destroy in more ways than one and that we need to control it or we miss out on a lot. One woman said that she hears much today about how it's okay to be angry and that we should let anger out, but "we've forgotten how destructive anger can be if you let it out incorrectly." A retired man of sixty-five claims that "anger is the most dangerous of all emotions." He thinks it can be devastating to the individual as well as the community—even the whole world. A seventy-year-old man stresses that it's good to let anger out as long as it is done in the right way. Also, there are times one should never get angry, like when drinking or after a big disappointment, because "anger can be devastating when not handled properly." He said that he saw this a lot, such as when people bump somebody else's car and get shot for it.

Remembering her own experience, one woman said, "I have never understood crimes of passion until some of what I've been through has happened to me and I understand it now—like absolutely losing control and wanting to beat the hell out of somebody." This woman never thought of herself as violent. She believes that suppressed emotion is the problem; sooner or later, a trigger comes along, and "you erupt like a volcano and lose control and almost don't know what you're doing." This woman is working on her anger style and said with a deprecating smile that she would like to practice what she is preaching—to do something about the things that bother her *before* they overwhelm her. A woman in her forties describes anger as "this dark that comes over me." She talked about having people in her life who have "just about driven me crazy" and she and a friend get together to pray for these people. This is her way of dissipating the feelings of anger. "You can't stay mad when you pray for them!" she relays with a smile.

The importance of letting anger out was mentioned by several men and several women. A thirty-five-year-old white woman said, "You have to get it out. People who hold it in are in trouble." A forty-two-year-old mother of two has learned that it is better to blow off short bouts of steam rather than let it build up. She also stresses that it is important to bring resolution to wounds. She sees anger as natural but also pointed out the need to channel and control it. She finds that the world in general is "losing its gracious spirit."

A fifty-four-year-old man discussed how important it is for him to get his anger out because, as he put it, he "doesn't carry anger well." It affects everything—his eating, thinking, his everyday life. He is not recommending fighting with someone or hurting them but stresses the importance of talking about the anger feelings. A young man feels that it is important to share anger feelings but admonishes that just because you express how you feel doesn't necessarily improve the situation. One must be careful about what is shared and how it is shared. A very thoughtful man in his early fifties believes strongly that if you internalize too much of the anger—"if you just eat it"—you are putting yourself at risk. Find somebody to talk with about your anger or think it through. Also realize that anger is cumulative. He thinks back to his childhood and realizes that he was taught to hold anger in and deal with it on his own, but without being told how to do this. So we learn how to hide anger and spend half of our life figuring out why we are not supposed to do that. "If you kick a dog," he says, "he snarls, which is normal, but a human being is not supposed to do that." It takes us a while to figure out how to deal with anger in an open, constructive way.

From listening to these individuals, it became clear that anger had a lot of different meanings for them. One middle-aged professional man believes that there is a direct correlation between anger and the need to control, so that if you could deal with the underlying control problems, a lot of anger would go away. A man with a similar background said that anger represents some sort of hurt and that he has heard that if you scratch the surface of anger, you find depression. In his own life, he has noticed this association. When his marriage broke up and his wife took the children and moved away, he experienced depression. He finds that when he does get angry, depression often follows. For that reason, he tries not to get angry because he knows what comes with it. Another man explained that he saw anger as "the emotional equivalent of a pain receptor in the skin." Thus, when he gets angry, he acknowledges that something is wrong—"something in my environment is either fixing to hurt me or is hurting me. Now what is it, and how do I take control?" Anger then becomes a useful cue. This man has learned not to let anger overwhelm him, whether it comes from within or from someone else. When someone else vents his or her anger at him, he uses the Japanese concept of *mushin*, which means "empty mind," as a way to "go around" and "adapt to" the situation at hand. The idea is to become like water, which moves around any obstacle. A man in his fifties thinks that anger results when people don't do things the way they were supposed to have done them. Thus, they are really angry at themselves most of the time but don't want to take blame or responsibility for what went wrong. He related the story of his son who had left a radar detector in his convertible. It was subsequently stolen, and the son got extremely angry. He was really angry at *himself*, according to the father, because he left the detector in a place where it could be seen instead of locking it into the trunk. A couple of individuals, one male and the other female, talked about the relationship between anger and our own state of mind. The man put it this way: "You got to get your house cleared up before you can mess with somebody else's." He stresses that if you are angry and disappointed with yourself, you tend to get a lot more angry at somebody else.

A couple of women raised the issue of using anger as a way to abdicate responsibility. A professional woman who works with people who are in stressful relationships said that she has learned that anger or the lack of control of anger is used as an excuse to do a lot of bad things because you can come back and say, "I'm sorry. I lost my temper." People often use anger as a justification for being hurtful or irresponsible, said the other woman, and then say later, "I was mad," as though that makes it all right.

The importance of being able to talk to each other, the need to forgive others for hurting you or angering you, and the need to learn more about anger were also brought up. "Our society has mixed-up ideas about anger," said a middle-aged professional woman. "There is a folk belief that when you are angry, you've got to express it. Some things we do to dissipate anger may actually fuel it."

A couple of men, one in his seventies and one in his forties, advise us either not to get angry at all or, if we must get angry, at least get it over with quickly. The older man said, "Avoid anger at all costs; it'll only get you into trouble. Forget about it and walk away." The younger man reminds us that "it's very rarely ever worth it!" He thinks that anger almost never accomplishes what you want, given the time and effort it takes. He talked about his wife's getting angry and then staying angry for perhaps three days—a big price to pay. His own attitude is, "Let's hash it out right now in the next ten or fifteen minutes and then go on to the next thing."

A woman who has thought a lot about anger as part of her job offers several insights. She sees anger as a basic emotion that is a "cover feeling" for needs that are not being met, an indicator that something needs to be worked on. She urges people not to act out of anger because it really hurts others as well as oneself. It is important to listen to it and to use it as a motivator but one should not dump it on somebody, especially if you have more power and authority than the other person. She credits the book *When Anger Hurts* for providing the insight that most problems are caused by a combination of stressed feelings and a record in the head ("It's all his fault!"). Thus, we have to reduce our stress *and* turn off the record. She also talked about anger being a spiral and that at some point one hits the point of no return and loses control. At this point, there is no rationality, and there is no use trying to talk rationally to this person; one needs to wait until the anger is spent. This woman also talked about children and anger and aggression and how it is necessary to teach them anger management (don't go up "Anger Mountain"; instead go down "Talk-It-Out Trail") long before they grow up.

Most of their suggestions are in line with both ancient and modern wisdom, and many of these thoughts on anger are reflected in the research literature. People like Carole Tavris, Albert Ellis, Aaron Beck, and many others have discussed the importance of understanding anger rather than just expressing it. For example, by simply reframing a situation, our anger dissipates or at least decreases. Tavris (1989) provides a list of "anger-arousing" and "anger-reducing perceptions" and "anger-intensifying" and "cooling-off habits" in her book. Basically, feeling justifiably wronged ("I deserve better than this") or blaming ("It's your fault!") make us more angry. Thoughts such as "Bad things happen" or "She couldn't help it," the use of humor, and feeling empathy for the other person will dissipate anger. Yelling, accusing, pouting, and plotting revenge tend to intensify our anger, while counting to ten, sleeping on it, exercise, or distraction allow us to feel less angry. Beck (1988), like some of the respondents, talks about anger being comparable to pain as a survival strategy. In fact, he states that the word *anger* derives from roots meaning "trouble, affliction, or pain." Thus anger is a signal that alerts us to a problem.

SUGGESTIONS FOR IMPROVING MALE-FEMALE RELATIONSHIPS

Respondents were asked to share their thoughts on what could be done to improve relations between women and men. In order to get at what people thought was most important, they were first asked, "If there was one thing that you could change about the way women and men relate to each other today, what would it be?" As a follow-up question, I asked for additional suggestions for improvement. As I listened to their answers, I was struck by the thoughtfulness expressed by these individuals.

More than half of the women's and the men's answers focused on the need to understand and communicate with each other better. There was wistfulness in many voices and faces as they talked about the need for women and men to be more open with each other, to be better listeners, to talk to each other, to understand each other. "Just to have men and women talk to each other, not accuse each other, to talk levelheadedly. We might find out what the other person is thinking." This woman went on to mention "preconceived notions" where we assume "he did this and she did this because..." and the "because" may not be right. It is possible, she says, that we attribute a lot of motives to other people that have nothing to do with what is really going on; "we might just miss the whole boat and be angry over something that never really happened that way!" In a similar vein, another woman exclaimed, "I want the door to understanding to be opened. Each needs to know what the other is really like instead of making generalizations. I don't know that much about the male. I don't even know that much about the female!" Several others put in a plea for open, honest communication between the sexes. "Open communication. Say whatever you think! Men don't tell you the truth," laments one woman. A young, single, black woman said with conviction: "I'd make it so that everybody would automatically speak everything that comes to their mind. I think that a lot of problems come from that men and women don't talk enough; we don't share enough. The men say 'we're men,' and the women say 'we're women,' and we're different. That is true, we are different, but nobody is making an attempt to understand *why* you're different and why I'm different. We just deal with the differences and accept them. Where do we go from here? Do we just accept the differences? I mean, we got to get along." This feeling of differences as an obstacle was mentioned by another woman who wishes that we could just sit down and discuss issues and feel as if we understand each other. However, she says that "men don't understand women's emotions. Men have a hard shell because they go out and work; men have a hard time relating to women on a softer, more emotional scale; they don't hear us."

As one way to get over these differences, another woman recommends that "a man needs to be a woman and a woman needs to be a man!" If only we could switch with each other temporarily! A slightly more realistic proposal was made by another woman who stressed that we need to understand that men and women are not the same and that we think about things differently. Therefore, we need to put ourselves in the other's place so we can understand each other more. She feels that a lot of anger arises out of our inability to understand the other sex. Another woman said that the answer to improved understanding is "to focus on the personhood and similarities." She stated that he may be a male, but he's a person; she may be a female, but she's a person. Our stereotypes may get in the way because it is possible that men may be more tender and more easily hurt than women. "Just because someone is big, strong, and masculine doesn't mean that we should discount their emotions even though men haven't allowed themselves to be emotional." Another woman said with frustration, "Get the other to open up. People basically don't talk anymore—not men and women, younger people with older people, black with white." She recommends that we write out a weekly list on how to communicate. One woman says very simply: "If you both don't know what the other is thinking, there's no way you can improve the relationship."

Many of these sentiments were echoed by the men. "Fostering an environment where men and women talk to each other and say what they mean— no games, no hidden agendas, nothing unsaid and also it being perceived on both parts, but particularly women, that what one says is what they mean!" To reiterate the last part of his message, this man used the example of his birthday when his wife asked him what he wanted to do. He answered, "Nothing," and told her why. She would not accept that he really wanted to do nothing and continued to ask him several more times in different ways what he "really" wanted. He got very frustrated because he meant what he said the first time, but she would not leave it alone. This frustration eventually leads to anger. He feels that this situation recurs with other women who won't "leave it alone" and won't accept what a man says at face value. Another man urged "open, honest communication so that we could talk about everything." Another man sought to make men and women honest because, he believes, most people, if they act in good faith, can handle honesty. He stated that dishonesty has a life of its own. Honesty is always heading toward a good source; it may hurt for the moment like a flu shot, but if you don't get the flu, that's good, and it was worth the temporary pain.

A middle-aged, married father of two suggested "some kind of mechanism to teach people how to communicate." This mechanism could be a course or a workbook of some kind. He made an analogy of how he got his professional degree in a health-related field and then went into business for himself but without having learned anything about running a business. Similarly, men and women get married without ever having learned how to run a marriage. He stressed that courtship is "a fake environment" and that if you had to maintain the same intensity (emotionally, physically, financially) in marriage, you'd last only a year. He and his wife actually did more than most other people by talking to a minister before marriage, but "it was a joke." A friend of his had a workbook to go through with his intended and said it helped them tremendously. An elderly man, retired, married, and a father of three, said with emphasis that "people don't even begin to touch the tremendous importance of knowing how to express yourself. They have no idea of the benefits that can accrue—the touching, the talking." He gave an example of how much the simple act of stopping to pick a flower by the roadside on the way home can mean to someone. This simple act takes little effort and costs nothing and yet it will reap great rewards of appreciation and deepened feelings of love.

In the spirit of improving communication between the sexes, several men recommended tampering with gender categories. As one man put it, "It's going to sound stupid, but change all men to think like women, or else change all women to think like men." He thinks that the makeup of the sexes is so different that there will always be some problems. He doesn't know which is better: to have all men more like women or vice versa. Another man said we need to be able to allow women the sensation of being a man and vice versa, to walk in their shoes and feel the same pressures, many of which we don't talk about. He believes that there are emotions that men have that women never experience, and vice versa. When pressed for examples, he couldn't identify them. He laughed and said that if we proceeded to follow his recommendation, we might find out more than we want to know and start a world war!

The women gave a variety of other answers in answer to this question, but only two were shared by two or more people. A few people stressed the need to spend more time together. "It's a go-go society. The family needs to be the number one priority. If you spend more time together, you'll know what they are going through." She recommended that people turn off the television, play games together, have a "family night," go on more vacations, and talk to each other more. We pay too much attention to things, said another, and not enough to the people in our lives. A couple of other women felt that it is important to preserve and appreciate differences between women and men. One woman urged us "to appreciate the giftings and nature of women and men individually and collectively." She said that some of us are organizers, some servants, and some can clarify things; we have different strengths. The need for more trust, more equality, less violence, and greater commitment was mentioned. One woman had a somewhat unique view: she thinks we should educate men and women not to expect anything from each other but only to give to each other. Men being more caring and nurturing, women respecting themselves more, and both helping each other more in a "productive partnership" were three other suggestions. Finally, a woman argued that her one wish is to make it so that sex and romance are equally important to both sexes. Right now, sex is more important to men and romance is more important to women, and she thinks this creates a lot of problems.

Besides improved communication and understanding, the next most commonly mentioned suggestion on the part of men was to base one's life on Christ. Experiencing God, it is argued, would lead to improvement in all human relationships. The rest of the suggestions were made by individual men. These men urged us to compromise, to be "best friends," to be unselfish, to get rid of the idea that one is smarter than the other, to teach men to respect women. One man recommended getting rid of monogamy because it's a totally unrealistic concept. He believes polygamy would make for much better relationships. Another said we must address the confusion and frustration men and women feel by raising their consciousness and awareness. We need to let people know how things used to be and how they have changed and how these changes have created problems. We need to know that it's okay to feel confused, and we need to talk about feelings. One man said that we need to "let nature take care of itself—that's the way people should be living." He is upset because people are always trying to change everything they get their hands on. One man said he was not sure what the one thing would be, and another said that he really couldn't think of a thing that he would change: "God knew what He was doing when He made men and women."

When asked for additional suggestions, four women and ten men had nothing else to add. Of those who did, the biggest category again was improving communication. One woman stressed that we need to share our feelings even if they're negative, or else anger builds, and "then you don't care anymore and just want to let anger out." By this point it is rage. Reading John Gray's book, *Men Are from Mars and Women Are from Venus*, was recommended by one woman. "If we could talk to each other!" said one older woman. She said that her husband has cancer and yet they don't talk to each other about it. "I just can't!" she said with anguish. A young woman who is already divorced thinks that every married couple should go to a marriage counselor, whether they have problems or not. Anger starts with "a little teeny pea, and if you don't talk about it, it snowballs into a big deal and then it's hard to deal with."

One man believes that it is extremely important to be able to speak your mind. He told a story about himself and his wife when they were first married. Early in his marriage he said he forgot that his wife had a life before she met him, that she had her own dreams and goals. He figured that now that she had him, what else could she want? She became more quiet and withdrawn as time went on. One day they were driving somewhere and he felt strongly that something was wrong. He stopped the car on the interstate and asked her what was on her mind. She broke down and cried and to his shock, he found out that she was deeply troubled about a lot of things. She told him that everything had happened too quickly; they had gotten married, moved to a new place, and had a baby. In all of this, what had been her passion in life, her music, had gotten lost. Upon hearing this, he encouraged her to go back to school, and she now has an undergraduate degree in music. He wonders what would have happened to them if he had not insisted on her sharing her feelings. This man remembered that his own mother had "lived for his dad" and had sacrificed all her personal dreams, and her husband had not even appreciated it.

Both sexes mentioned the importance of setting priorities. One woman exclaimed, "Men and women want to have it all! You can't put 100 percent in everything! Sometimes relationships have to take priority if they're going to survive." Showing appreciation and care was also seen as helpful in making relationships better. An elderly man advises "being a sparkplug!" This means saying something nice or appreciative, making eye contact, and doing anything that conveys the feeling of caring. Being more open-minded was also mentioned by both sexes, and they made comments that included: "look at each other as people; forget about gender as much as you can"; "don't prejudge people"; "explore both differences and common ground." The importance of treating each other as equals and being more patient was stressed by both women and men.

Several women talked about the importance of "a good dose of God." One of them credits the success of her marriage to the presence of God in her life. When she first got married, she would get angry if there was a mess in the living room and she would carry this anger inside. Today she has patience and forgiveness; she now realizes that men don't see things the way women do and instead of getting angry, she simply asks her husband to pick up the mess (which he does gladly). She commented that she saw her mother stay mad at her father all her life and she didn't want to repeat this in her marriage. The need to have empathy was also brought up by a couple of women. We don't know the stresses the other goes through, says one; therefore we must put ourselves into their shoes.

Many one-time suggestions were given by both men and women but mostly the women, since ten men had no further ideas for improving relationships. "Don't carry baggage from a previous relationship," admonished one man; "less fixation on sex," said another; "be more trusting and more submissive," said two other men.

The remaining suggestions from the women included mutual respect, to have faith that we can understand each other, and to abide by the golden rule. "Do nice things for yourself when in an anger situation," advised one woman; "compromise and sacrifice and be more committed to the relationship," said two more. One woman talked about not taking things for granted; she believes that 90 percent of a male-female relationship is a rut. Get rid of the television set and have a "black-out time" urged another, who thinks that we don't have enough time together as a family. Embrace the differences rather than fight them says another; there can be strength in these differences, she believes. The last comment came from a woman who feels that we need to give more attention and care to our relationships: "I think we're put on this earth to learn about relationships; I think that's what it's all about. I think that's how we grow personally, how we mature, how we give back to other people. Relationships are the key to personal growth."

As I was listening to the answers to these questions, it struck me how wise and wonderful so many of them were. I have come across many of them in the textbooks I use to teach courses on marriage and the family. It was clear that many of these individuals had learned the value of these goals and suggestions from personal and often painful experience. It was also obvious that some of these suggestions were unrealistic. How many of their suggestions were actually put to good use I cannot tell.

SIGNIFICANT LEARNINGS

After finishing the interviews, I asked myself what was most surprising, most troublesome, most insightful, and most hopeful about what I had heard. One of the most surprising and troublesome findings was how few of these individuals ever had anyone teach them anything systematic and useful about anger, one of the most powerful emotions in our human repertoire. Most respondents remembered no specific efforts on the part of their parents to help them recognize, understand, and constructively deal with feelings of anger—despite the fact that many of the families were marked by conflict and anger. Most likely, these parents had no clue themselves about how to tame this difficult emotion. It was interesting that about twice as many women as men remembered being talked to about anger during their childhood.   Brody and Hall (1993) reviewed literature that shows that generally parents discuss emotions more with their daughters than with their sons *except* in the case of anger, which is supposedly discussed more with sons.

We are known as homo sapiens—the wise ones, the discerning ones, the ones characterized by our ability to think. We tend to forget that we are also the feeling ones, the passionate ones. Much of our upbringing is geared to stimulating and improving our capacity for thought processes of various kinds and to hiding and curbing our emotions. We don't seem to trust our minds to confront and deal with our emotions openly. We implicitly and explicitly receive the message that our emotional side is troublesome, dangerous, and unsettling. We rarely hear someone threatening "to get thinking," but we often hear someone threatening "to get angry." Ironically, we probably have created as many messy situations by faulty thinking as by expressing negative emotions. Emotions such as anger are scary because we see a direct connection or link between the anger and possible hurt. Yet the link between twisted, illogical thinking and possible hurt may be no less tangible, though perhaps less immediate and gut level. The point is that we need to be taught to "feel things through" as much as to "think things through." Both processes are vital to our well-being and survival. We have set up a situation where we define reasoning as the opposite of emoting, where one or the other has to be in control at any given time.

Most of the people I interviewed did not have the benefit of having someone sit down with them and talk about feelings—what they mean, when they are appropriate, how to manage them. This does not mean that they did not learn any lessons about anger. It just means that they learned many destructive things by observing parents and siblings who didn't understand much about anger either. Many of them learned to hide their feelings as they saw what inappropriate ways of sharing anger could do or because they learned that anger is unacceptable. Many more men than women exploded verbally or physically.   Many of the respondents were exposed to extreme reactions when it came to anger. Family members tended either to keep conflictual feelings hidden or expressed them in a rather explosive fashion.   Few of their significant others had a style of anger expression that was somewhere in-between.   These findings are consistent with what people in general do.   Strong, DeVault, and Sayad (1998) claim that most people have learned to manage anger by either venting it or suppressing it; both are very destructive.   These authors encourage people to view anger as a warning sign that must be acknowledged in order to go to the source of what is wrong.

The research consistently reports stereotypical perceptions of women's and men's anger styles, with women being seen as more reserved with anger than men. This pattern was found clearly with the parents of these respondents.   Overall, the mothers were quiet and withdrawn when upset, while the fathers typically yelled and screamed and sometimes used physical aggression.   The respondents themselves deviated somewhat from this pattern.   The differences in anger expression style between male and female respondents were not as great, although the men were somewhat more likely to be loud, explosive, and physical than the women.   Close to half of both sets of respondents remembered hiding feelings of anger.   Today, male and female respondents are very similar in that the majority of those who were quiet and withdrawn are trying to be more open and the majority of those who were loud and obnoxious are working on becoming more controlled. The sexes also converged in their feelings of comfort with their own anger, with most saying they are fairly or somewhat comfortable today.   They diverged in feelings about others' anger; the majority of the women said they were not comfortable when others were angry at them in comparison to half of the men feeling uncomfortable with other's anger.

Probably the area of greatest agreement between the sexes was in regard to ideal ways of expressing anger. Almost without exception, they all firmly believed that it is important to sit down and calmly (at least at some point) discuss the issues openly and clearly and without attacking the other.   Both men and women recognized the importance of discussing problematic issues rather than keeping their feelings inside. Karen Kayser, the author of *When Love Dies*, talks about the harmful impact of using avoidance for handling conflict; such partners become increasingly separate from each other. Of course, knowing what is the best thing to do is not the same as actually doing it, but as someone once put it, "Knowing is half the battle!"

I was surprised and disturbed to find so many individuals, both male and female, who had grown up with a father who was angry, hostile, abusive, or emotionally distant.   The encounters with these fathers left scars that are still healing today. Some may never heal. The only positive legacy these fathers left behind is that some of their sons and daughters resolved never to inflict such pain and confusion on their own families. Brody and Hall (1993) also write about different interaction styles of mothers and fathers, with fathers being more demanding, threatening, demeaning, and foul-mouthed. This negative demeanor was corroborated by the respondents' stories. This situation urgently needs to be explored further. I would not have expected so much trouble with extremely angry and sometimes violent fathers in this sample.   If I had deliberately interviewed specifically angry individuals, would their backgrounds have held even more destructive and distant relationships with fathers? The tales of the fathers make it clear how important it is to address powerful emotions such as anger and frustration, especially in a family setting, where the rest of the family members are in a physically and emotionally dependent relationship with each other. The father-child relationship is already strained by the lack of physical and emotional closeness that derives from relatively little father involvement in the child rearing process. It cannot afford to be further impaired by fathers who cannot or will not take control of their negative emotions.

I was taken aback by the strong and consistent negative stereotypes women cited when talking about what made them angry about other women. Over and over again I heard how insecure, untrustworthy, sneaky, manipulative, and back-stabbing women are. A lot of this negative behavior was seen as occurring in the context of women trying to establish relationships with men. Other women were seen as competitors. But even without men in the picture, women were seen as playing a lot of games in order to raise their rank regarding other women. Men in this sample seem to share the same concern when they complained that deceitful and manipulative women angered them. I was especially surprised by the perceived lack of self-esteem and self-respect that angered so many women. I had hoped that the women's movement and its emphasis on strength, competence, and independence had uprooted a lot of this old-fashioned insecurity. Are we really "our own worst enemy," as one of the respondents put it?

I was surprised that more individuals, especially women, did not raise division-of-labor issues as a source of anger. Given the publicity surrounding this issue and all the research that documents how unequal it is, I expected more women to be frustrated about the lack of help and more men about being expected to help. Not only did relatively few women mention this as a source of anger, but they also did not commonly perceive this as a source of anger for other women. Men also rarely identified this as a source of anger for either women or other men or themselves. Daphne Spain and Suzanne Bianchi, the authors of a recent book, *Balancing Act* (1996), give credence to this finding when they say, "Academic researchers seem more troubled by the division of household labor than the women they interview, many of whom think their household arrangement is equitable" (171). The authors point out that one's perception of fairness depends on a number of conditions, such as comparison of one's own status with that of others and gender ideology. For example, if a woman believes that it is her duty to do the housework regardless of her employment status, then she is not likely to complain. It could also be that a lack of sharing on part of the men does not generate anger but something milder, like irritation or annoyance. The results could also be an artifact of the sample characteristics. Many of the women were in their thirties and forties and presumably have addressed this issue and solved it, resigned themselves to this undesirable situation, or have left the situation. The fact that many of these women were born and raised in the South could also have a bearing, since the South is more conservative than the rest of the country and thus women are more likely to feel that housework is their duty.

Several noteworthy differences based on sex emerged in reference to sources and extent of anger. Generally women were much more certain about their own and others' feelings of anger. For example, when women were asked to judge other women's anger toward men or men's anger toward women, most had no trouble stating their opinion. Men were much more unsure about women's anger toward men but more sure about other men's anger than women's anger. The same pattern held for their own feelings of anger. Almost all the women had definite opinions on what made them angry about men. A sizable number of men either were not sure what made them angry or could think of nothing that angered them. Not only did women come up with more grievances; they had much more consensus on anger sources than the men who were much more individualistic (perhaps less stereotyped) in their judgments. Generally the women had no problems thinking of things that angered them about the men in their lives, men in general, or other women for that matter.

The responses given by this group of women and men uphold findings from my own previous research as well as from some of the other research findings that identified women as the angrier sex. This pattern holds for anger in general as well as gender-based anger. Higher proportions of women than men said they get angry "a lot" when asked about anger generally. More women than men said they got angry "a lot" at both people they know and people in general. Both verbally and nonverbally, the women generally communicated greater anger intensity than the men did.

An interesting sex difference emerged in regard to the type of issues respondents got most upset about. As a group, the men became more intense and agitated when they talked about some of the general gender-related changes in our society. In contrast, women tended to get more visibly aroused and upset about what specific people in their lives had done to them. There were quite a few men who strongly voiced their opposition to affirmative action or quotas or women in the military or women who "should" be staying home with their children but could think of nothing that angered them about specific women in their lives. This suggests that women are more unhappy about activities on the home front, while men are more disturbed by what is happening in the social realm, especially the work front.

In regard to sources of anger, there were no simple patterns. In answering, "Why are women angry at men?" four different sources were drawn on: the women's own feelings in regard to men they know, the women's feelings in regard to men in general, the women's perceptions of why other women are angry, and the men's perceptions of why women are angry. A wide variety of answers were given. There was a fair amount of consistency in the anger sources for both groups of men. However, the explanations tended to incorporate more structural factors as the reference point became less personal. All four viewpoints stress lack of sensitivity and understanding as a major source of anger for women. Issues related to inequality, especially in the workplace, comprise a second major source of anger (it was represented in three out of the four standpoints—all except "men they know"). Lack of responsibility turned out to be an important source of anger from the women's perspectives but was not perceived to be important from the men's viewpoint. There was a similar lack of congruence for several other anger sources as well: sexual issues (sexual fixation, sexual abuse) and physical and emotional aggression, with women thinking they're important sources of anger but not men.

In answer to the question, "Why are men angry at women?" we find little consensus among the men in reference to women they know. They named a lot of personal attributes that no more than two or three men agreed on. There was more consensus when they thought about women in general who angered them because they were insensitive, irresponsible, and deceitful and manipulative. What angered men personally tended to be quite different from what they saw as other men's sources of anger. Although men themselves are frustrated by rigid, deceitful, insensitive women (among many other traits), they believe that other men's biggest source of anger derives from women's changing roles. These changes are seen as threatening and confusing men in various ways. A secondary source of anger identified for men was lack of sensitivity and understanding, and this source of anger is more similar to the kinds of things men complain about from their own perspective.

It was somewhat surprising to find more men than women voicing concern about the welfare of children in society. This was men's number one dislike about current social conditions. This is quite clearly an issue that women traditionally have thought and worried about. This finding may reflect women's and men's different comfort levels with gender role change generally. It is clear that women's roles have changed more than men's and that women consistently are more in favor of many gender-related changes than men are. It would be easier for women to support working outside the home even if that means other child care arrangements need to be made since women have fought long and hard for the right to earn their own money. It may also be harder for women to acknowledge problems that children are having since they are the ones held responsible, not the men. The *News and Observer* recently released findings from a survey that speak to this issue. Results show that "most people believe family life would be better if mothers could stay at home" (Morin and Rosenfeld 1998, 24A). This view was shared by women and men, with half of college-educated professional women agreeing. These results imply that women and men are equally worried about the fate of children; this was not reflected in my sample.

Analysis of respondents' thoughts on recent gender-related changes in our society revealed a mixture of convergence and divergence among women and men. Women overwhelmingly praised greater opportunities and choices that are now available to them. This was followed by greater equality, more power, and independence. All of these speak to a world that is perceived to be opening up and expanding. The men's best-liked change was greater equality between women and men followed by more flexible roles and then new perspectives and challenges, which tied with men being forced to change. There was some overlap between the men's and the women's lists, with both expressing appreciation for greater equality. On the negative side, what women disliked the most about recent social changes and conditions is the blurring of gender roles (which includes the movement of women into inappropriate places) and the loss of moral bearings. Again, the concerns voiced by the men overlapped to some extent with those given by the women. The men complained about children being neglected, women in the military, government interference, and people trying to get rid of differences between the sexes. Clearly both are quite concerned about men's and women's nature and proper place. By and large, these individuals wanted to maintain distinct differences between the sexes, even though they overwhelmingly supported equal rights and opportunities. Although they could visualize women in most job settings and men taking on household and child care duties, they wanted to preserve essential masculine and feminine qualities.

IMPLICATIONS

Through answers to various questions it became clear that women are the angrier sex. They expressed more anger in reference to general issues as well as gender-specific ones. It's one thing for women to be angrier than men and for men to realize this, and another for women to be angrier and men not perceive this. The latter situation was reflected in my findings. While the majority of women felt there are a lot of angry women (as well as a lot of men), the majority of men felt that a lot of men in our society are angry at women, but when it came to how women felt, they either were not sure, or felt they were not angry, or they were divided on this issue. Thus men and women are in agreement about males' anger being a common problem, but they diverge when it comes to feelings about women being angry. The pattern for personalized anger was also different for women and men. More women said they get angry "a lot" at men (especially those they know) than men said this about women. Thus, women see themselves and other women as angry, while men see other men as angry but not themselves. Each sex has some misperceptions. Men need to realize that there is more anger on the part of women than they think, and women need to realize that men are not that angry at women in their lives.

Men and women seemed to share an understanding in regard to what angers men in general about women in general because women also identified women's changing roles as a major source of anger for men. There is some congruence also about anger and women in general since both women and men referred to lack of equality and lack of understanding or support as being anger sources for these women.

The largest perception gap is between what women and men say makes them angry personally and what the other sex thinks angers them. For example, women say they get angry at men who are irresponsible, domineering, insensitive, noncommunicative, sexually exploitative, condescending, and too aggressive and who treat them unfairly in the workplace. However, when men try to guess why women are angry, they pick up on only a couple of these complaints (lack of equality and lack of sensitivity or understanding). Men say they get angry at women who are irresponsible, insensitive, and deceitful and manipulative, but women think that men get angry at women because of the changes associated with women's roles. Thus, there seems to be a considerable gap in perception in regard to sources of anger. Perhaps this study will help to raise the awareness levels of both sexes.

The findings suggest some problems in sharing feelings of anger. Most of the men indicated that they would not be as open and honest with a woman as with a man. Although their motivation was benign—they wanted to keep women from getting too upset—the consequences may not be. If we believe it is important to share feelings honestly, especially in regard to conflicting issues, then women may not be getting very accurate messages about what troubles men. In an effort to be kind and protective, men are keeping women from understanding them fully. On the other hand, women say they usually don't modify their anger expression based on the person's sex but on the basis of the type of relationship they have with the person. Thus, men may not hear what is really on a woman's mind unless she feels comfortable and trusting with him.

The fact that both women and men overwhelmingly believe that men and women are different when it comes to aspects of anger should alert both sexes to the fact that there may be a lot of potential misunderstandings. Neither should assume anything about the other except that each *will* experience anger and that neither particularly likes others being angry at them. Tread carefully when the grounds are full of anger! Both need to sharpen their communication skills. As Tavris (1989) warns, "You and your target must speak the same anger language" because anger is a form of communication and whether it works depends on whether the message is received.

The findings point out the great importance that both women and men place on being treated with sensitivity and understanding. It is clear from these interviews that women and men need to pay more attention to each other's needs and vulnerabilities. Both sexes also strongly resent condescending and controlling behaviors. Neither men nor women want to be treated as though they are inferior and as though someone else has the right to tell them what to do. All of my previous studies lend support to the important role that lack of understanding, domineering and controlling behaviors, and condescending attitudes play in generating feelings of anger.

Men need to hear the message that women are sending about irresponsibility. This was mentioned more than any other complaint about the men in their lives. Since I began working on this project, my ears are always tuned in to anger-related sound waves. I have had many informal conversations with various individuals on topics related to this book. In fact, some conversations started because I was writing this book. Although I was somewhat surprised to find so many women in this sample upset about men who are irresponsible, I find that over and over again this theme is voiced in other contexts. I have heard acquaintances and friends bemoan the fact that all the good men were taken or that there just aren't very many of them. And "good" men are defined to a large extent as men you can count on, men who are not afraid of commitment, men who have your welfare at heart. In a recent class discussion on work and family roles and the conflicts generated by them, I suggested that one way to ease this tension was to choose carefully the man you will marry, and one young black woman said with exasperation, "But where do I find such a man?" She claimed that sometimes men act fine when you are dating them, but as soon as you walk down the church aisle, they change and are no longer willing to share all the work that needs to be done. Within minutes, several other women in the class chimed in with the same complaints. As I am working on this book, our society is witnessing the phenomenon of the Promise Keepers. I am inclined to believe that a major reason for women's support of this movement is their frustration with irresponsible men. There doesn't seem to be the same level of discontent on the part of men. They are either finding more of what they are looking for or are not as willing to share their concerns.

The central role played by irresponsible, controlling, and insensitive, nonsupportive behaviors and actions is reinforced by what Kayser (1993) found in her book on why people fall out of love. The couples she interviewed for this book identified those same traits as being the major "turning-point events" that changed their positive feelings for their partners to negative ones.

Along the same lines, it is clear that both women and men feel strongly about the role of better communication in improving relations among them. This came out in both the cross-sex comparisons and the answers to the question, "What could we do to improve relations between women and men?" Although communication problems were one of the sources of anger identified by women and men, it was clearly not seen as the most serious one. Yet in thinking about improving relationships between the sexes, better communication overwhelmingly dominated the responses. People wanted the sexes to talk more to each other, to be more open and honest, and to be more willing to understand each other. Relatively few people thought about the conditions that might allow or encourage improved communication. Those who did tended to give unrealistic answers, such as women becoming men and men becoming women for a while. Such a solution does indicate the urgent desire to have each sex be able to see the world from the other's viewpoint. Interestingly enough, even though so many stressed communication as either a problem or a solution, many people wanted to preserve distinctions between men's and women's roles and personalities. The two seem to be somewhat contradictory impulses.

Several of the sources of anger seem to be associated with traditional gender role expectations, especially on the part of men. What the women in all of these studies are saying repeatedly is that they no longer accept and tolerate domineering, condescending, inequitable, and physically and sexually abusive or exploitative behaviors and attitudes. It would seem appropriate to stop teaching men that they are superior or privileged in any way in regard to women, that they have a right to hoist their sexual desires on women, and that it is masculine to be either physically or emotionally aggressive. Instead, let us teach men to be more communicative, sensitive, and responsible. On the other hand, it also behooves us to encourage women to be more competent, secure, and sensitive, and less manipulative and deceitful.

It is hopeful that so many men are angered by sexist, disrespectful, stereotypic treatment of women. They see such behavior in the men they know as well as men in general. Perhaps they will work toward eliminating these attitudes and behaviors in themselves and others, thus eliminating several of women's sources of anger.

I don't want to distort the picture. In terms of my overall impression, I believe that many of these individuals seem to have more problems with anger in general than with gender-based anger specifically. By and large, the women and men I interviewed seemed content with the significant others in their lives but more troubled with people and conditions around them. There were relatively few intensely unhappy or angry individuals in the group. There *were* many individuals who got frustrated and irritated with their spouses, dating partners, children, and friends. However, when they get angry, the concerns listed above seem to be the most significant ones.

Although I did not interview many nonwhite men and women, based on the few interviews and on informal discussions with others, there is reason to believe that some of the issues and ways of dealing with them may be very different. Several black women expressed strong feelings on the subject of black men dating white women. With great disdain, they hypothesized that black men dated white women or wanted to date white women because white women are more willing to be bossed around and otherwise mistreated by black men. Thus, these black women see black men as being unhappy and resentful toward black women, who are perceived as too independent and too critical of their ways. A short article by Brooks (1997), "Why Are Black Men Angry?" presents the views of eleven black men of different ages and occupational background, and one of the men addresses this issue and confirms the black women's perceptions. One of these men, a twenty-four-year-old recording artist named Rome, said that black men marry out of their race because "the white woman provided him with less grief and problems as far as his home life is concerned" (66). Among other ones, racial dimensions are ripe for exploration in regard to gender-based anger.

I'd like to think that the younger generation coming of age today will make the phrase "the battle of the sexes" obsolete. I'm inclined to think that it may take a little longer. Lamanna and Riedman (1991) state that gender conflict and tension will increase before it gets better. A survey by *Self* magazine ("He Vs She" 1992) showed that 41 percent of the married and 43 percent of the unmarried women strongly agreed with the statement that "increasing equality between men and women will inevitably increase conflict between them." Some argue that a lot of these problems will go away as the younger generation casts off traditional assumptions. However, a recent, nationwide New York Times/CBS poll of 1,055 teenagers indicates that their views on gender roles may continue to raise tensions. For example, the boys were substantially more traditional than the girls in their family and job expectations, with only 7 percent of the girls saying they expected to stay home after marriage and 19 percent of the boys expecting their future wives to stay home. Around one-third of the sample felt that males had more advantages today than females. A majority of the boys said that most of the boys they knew considered themselves better than girls. Most of the girls, however, said that the girls they knew saw boys as their equals.

Nevertheless, I look to the day when a male can relate to a female in such a way that he never feels a sense of superiority and no woman will ever belittle herself based on the accident of birth. In a conversation with a writer, actress Katharine Hepburn once said that she doubts "if men and women really suit each other.... They should live next door—and just visit now and then." Perhaps we will have to take her suggestion more seriously.

We have come to think of the family as a place (perhaps the only place) where we can relax and be ourselves, as one place where our emotions can run full play, where we can share all or most of our feelings. On the other hand, we also expect our family to be the place where we receive love, support understanding, and respect. As long as we're dealing with positive emotions such as joy and hope, it is easy to reconcile these two major goals. However, when it comes to what we call the "negative" emotions, such as fear and anger, the more we relax and freely share them, the less likely we are to garner respect, love, and support (at least given our cultural context). Angry people are not lovable, huggable, or even comfortable to be around. They are bad, scary, and dangerous, or at least obnoxious. Unfortunately, the family is a place where anger boils to the surface quite frequently and often in violent ways, and thus anger is a common emotion in this context.

One way to deal with uncomfortable, scary things is to ignore them or try to stay away from them. It seems that this is the path we have chosen as a culture when it comes to the negative emotions. It has struck me for a long time that in our years of growing up, many, if not most, of us miss out on some of the most important learnings of all: those involving the management of our emotions. Parents, teachers, and preachers take great pains to teach us how to walk and talk, and read and write, and how to be polite, clean, and successful. My point is not to disparage these teachings but to draw attention to all that we leave out. What were we taught about communication skills or conflict handling skills? Who teaches us how to recognize, express, and decrease anger? We are what we communicate. Who teaches us to translate that "I want to kill you!" often just means, "You really hurt me!" We will be told that the urge to kill and verbalizing such an urge is wrong and that we shouldn't feel that way and that we should go someplace and get ourselves under control. Meanwhile the underlying emotions are unacknowledged, probably misunderstood, and certainly not dealt with. How can we grow in emotionally healthy ways under such conditions? Eventually the nerve underneath the shiny white tooth rots and jeopardizes the whole tooth. I hope that reading this book will increase people's motivation to treat anger as a natural and critical emotion that needs attention and respect.

This project made me examine my own beliefs and habits when it comes to anger. There were many times when I started to lose my composure but would pull back because my mind played back some of the information and insight I had accumulated from reading material or talking to people. I am less likely to get lost in my anger now and more likely to step back and figure out what this anger signifies. I am keenly aware that harsh words, looks, and tones not only feed my own anger but the other person's as well, much as blowing on a fire causes it to flare up. You'll never catch me telling anyone, "You shouldn't be angry!" Instead I will try to understand what is being violated, what it is that is making a person angry. Someone once said that you cannot deny someone's feelings because they "just are." They are neither right nor wrong, good nor bad; they simply express a state of our being. They just *are*. To say to someone that he or she shouldn't feel that way is like saying the person shouldn't exist. However, it is appropriate, especially with negative emotions, to ask, "Why do you think you feel this way? What are the justifications for feeling this way? What made you feel this way? What are the consequences of feeling this way? If you don't like how you feel, what can be done to change the feeling?"

It is also important to teach people that feelings can change, that they don't have to control and overwhelm us. One of my favorite books is Kahlil Gibran's *The Prophet*. Among many wonderful passages is one on "reason and passion" where he affirms their importance and interdependence:

Your reason and your passion are the rudder and the sails of your seafaring soul. If either your sails or your rudder be broken, you can but toss and drift, or else be held at a standstill in mid-seas. For reason, ruling alone, is a force confining; and passion unattended, is a flame that burns to its own destruction. (50)

Anger left unattended can go out of control and be one of the most destructive forces around. But with the help of reason or thought, as well as new information, it can be used to move us forward into clearer and less troubled waters, where we can see our own and the other's reflection.

References

Allcorn, Seth. 1994. *Anger in the Workplace*. Westport, CT: Quorum Books.

Allis, Sam. 1990. "What Do Men Really Want?" *Time*, Fall.

Astrachan, Anthony. 1986. *How Men Feel*. Garden City, NY: Anchor Press.

Averill, James R. 1982. *Anger and Aggression: An Essay on Emotion*. New York: Springer-Verlag.

———. 1983. "Studies on Anger and Aggression: Implications for Theories of Emotion." *American Psychologist* 38:1145–62.

———. 1986. "The Acquisition of Emotions During Adulthood." In *The Social Construction of Emotions*, edited by Rom Harre. New York: Basil Blackwell.

———. 1993. "Illusions of Anger." In *Aggression and Violence*, edited by R. B. Felson and J. T. Tedeschi. Washington, D.C.: American Psychological Association.

Barefoot, J. C., et al. 1991. "Hostility Patterns and Health Implications: Correlates of Cook-Medley Hostility Scale Scores in a National Survey." *Health Psychology* 10:18–24.

Barefoot, John C. 1992. "Developments in the Measurement of Hostility." In *Hostility, Coping, and Health*, edited by Howard S. Friedman. Washington, D.C.: American Psychological Association.

Baron, Robert A. 1977. *Human Aggression*. New York: Plenum.

Baumeister, Roy F., Arlene Stillwell, and Sara R. Wotman. 1990. "Victim and Perpetrator Accounts of Interpersonal Conflict: Autobiographical Narratives About Anger." *Journal of Personality and Social Psychology* 59:994–1005.

Beck, Aaron. 1988. *Love Is Never Enough*. New York: Harper Perennial.

Berkowitz, Leonard. 1989. "Frustration-Aggression Hypothesis: Examination and Reformulation." *Psychological Bulletin* 106:59–73.

Bird, Gloria, and Keith Melville. 1994. *Families and Intimate Relationships*. New York: McGraw-Hill.

Black, Kathryn Stechert. 1990. "Can Getting Mad Get the Job Done?" *Working Woman*, March, 86–90.

Brody, Leslie R., and Judith A. Hall. 1993. "Gender and Emotion." In *Handbook of Emotions*, edited by Michael Lewis and Jeanette Haviland. New York: Guilford Press.

Brooks, Natasha. 1997. "Why Are Black Men Angry?" *Today's Black Woman*, September, 66–68.

Browne, Joy. 1997. "Managing Your Anger." *Dr. Joy Browne's Newsletter*, July, 6–7.

Buss, Arnold H. 1961. *The Psychology of Aggression*. New York: Wiley.

Buss, Arnold H., and Ann Durkee. 1957. "An Inventory for Assessing Different Kinds of Hostility." *Journal of Consulting Psychology* 21:343–49.

Campbell, Anne. 1993. *Men, Women, and Aggression*. New York: Basic Books.

Campbell, Anne, and Steven Muncer. 1987. "Models of Anger and Aggression in the Social Talk of Women and Men." *Journal for the Theory of Social Behavior* 17:489–511.

Campbell, Bebe Moore. 1986. *Successful Women, Angry Men: Backlash in the Two-Career Marriage*. New York: Random House.

Cancian, Francesca M., and Steven Gordon. 1988. "Changing Emotion Norms in Marriage: Love and Anger in U.S. Women's Magazines Since 1900." *Gender and Society* 2:308–42.

Chafetz, Janet Saltzman. 1989. "Marital Intimacy and Conflict: The Irony of Spousal Equality." In *Women: A Feminist Perspective*, edited by Jo Freeman. Palo Alto, CA: Mayfield.

Check, James V. P. 1988. "Hostility Toward Women: Some Theoretical Considerations." In *Violence in Intimate Relationships*, edited by G. W. Russell. New York: PMA Publishing Corporation.

Check, James V. P., and Neil M. Malamuth. 1985. "On Hostile Ground." *Psychology Today*, April, 56–61.

Clark, Margaret S., ed. 1992. *Emotion and Social Behavior*. Newbury Park, CA: Sage Publication.

Conroy, Pat. 1991. *The Prince of Tides*. New York: Bantam Books.

Cose, Ellis. 1995. "Black Men and Black Women." *Newsweek*, June 5, 66–69.

Crawford, June, and Susan Kippax. 1992. *Emotion and Gender*. Newbury Park, CA: Sage.

Denham, Gayle, and Kaye Bultemeier. 1993. "Anger: Targets and Triggers." In *Women & Anger*, edited by Sandra P. Thomas. New York: Springer Publishing Company.

Doyle, James A. 1989. *The Male Experience*. Madison, WI: Brown and Benchmark.

Edmunds, George G., and Donald C. Kendrick. 1980. *The Measurement of Human Aggressiveness*. New York: John Wiley and Sons.

Eisler, Richard M., and Jay R. Skidmore. 1987. "Masculine Gender Role Stress." *Behavior Modification* 2(2):123–36.

Eshleman, J. Ross. 1997. *The Family: An Introduction*. 8th ed. Boston: Allyn and Bacon.

Estrich, Susan. 1994. "Taking a Stand." *News and Observer* (Raleigh, NC), December 18.

Faludi, Susan. 1991. *Backlash*. New York: Crown.

Farley, Reynolds. 1996. *The New American Reality*. New York: Russell Sage Foundation.

Farrell, Warren. 1974. *The Liberated Man*. New York: Random House.

———. 1991. "Men as Success Objects." *Utne Reader*, May/June, 81–84.

Fein, Melvyn L. 1993. *I.A.M.: A Common Sense Guide to Coping with Anger*. Westport, CT: Praeger.

Franklin, Clyde W., II. 1989. "Black Male–Black Female Conflict: Individually Caused and Culturally Nurtured." In *Men's Lives: Readings in the Sociology of Masculinity*, edited by M. Kimmel and M. Messner. New York: Macmillan.

Freudenberger, Herbert J. 1987. "Today's Troubled Men." *Psychology Today*, December, 46–47.

Friedan, Betty. 1985. "Their Turn: How Men Are Changing." In *Marriage and Family*, edited by Leonard Cargan. Belmont, CA: Wadsworth.

Frodi, Ann. 1977. "Sex Differences in Perception of a Provocation: A Survey." *Perceptual and Motor Skills* 44:113–14.

———. 1978. "Experiential and Physiological Responses Associated with Anger and Aggression in Women and Men." *Journal of Research in Personality* 12:335–49.

Frodi, Ann, and Jacqueline Macaulay. 1977. "Are Women Always Less Aggressive Than Men? A Review of the Literature." *Psychological Bulletin* 84:634–60.

Gary, Lawrence E. 1986. "Predicting Interpersonal Conflict Between Men and Women." *American Behavioral Scientist* 29(5):635–46.

Gergen, Kenneth J., and Mary M. Gergen. 1988. "Narrative and the Self as Relationship." In *Advances in Experimental Social Psychology* (vol. 21, pp. 17–56), edited by Leonard Berkowitz. San Diego, CA: Academic Press.

Gibran, Kahlil. 1966. *The Prophet*. New York: Knopf.

Goleman, Daniel. 1995. *Emotional Intelligence*. New York: Bantam Books.

Gray, John. 1993. *Men, Women and Relationships*. Hillsboro, OR: Beyond Words Publishing, Inc.

Hacker, Helen. 1957. "The New Burdens of Masculinity." *Marriage and Family Living*, August, 227–33.

Harre, Rom, ed. 1986. *The Social Construction of Emotions*. New York: Basil Blackwell.

"He Vs She." 1992. *Self*, June, 140–43.

Hepburn, Katharine. "Newsmakers, 1997." *Newsweek*, May 5, 79.

Izard, Carroll E. 1991. *The Psychology of Emotions*. New York: Basil Blackwell.

Jeffers, Susan. 1989. *Opening Our Hearts to Men*. New York: Fawcett Columbine.

Kaylin, Lucy. 1994. "The Way We Are." *Gentlemen's Quarterly*, February, 118–21.

Kayser, Karen. 1993. *When Loves Dies*. New York: Guilford Press.

Kemper, Theodore D. 1978. *A Social Interactional Theory of Emotions*. New York: Wiley.

———. 1987. "How Many Emotions Are There? Wedding the Social and the Autonomic Components." *American Journal of Sociology* 93:263–89.

Kimbrell, Andrew. 1991. "A Time for Men to Pull Together." *Utne Reader*, May/June, 66–74.

Kimmel, Michael S., and Michael Messner, eds. 1989. *Men's Lives: Readings in the Sociology of Masculinity*. New York: Macmillan.

Kingma, Daphne Rose. 1993. *The Men We Never Knew: Women's Role in the Evolution of Gender*. Berkeley, CA: Conari Press.

Kipnis, Aaron, and Elizabeth Herron. 1994. *Gender War, Gender Peace*. New York: Morrow.

Kipnis, Aaron, and Elizabeth Hingston. 1993. "Ending the Battle Between the Sexes." *Utne Reader*, January/February, 69–76.

Kopper, Beverly A., and Douglas L. Epperson. 1991. "Women and Anger." *Psychology of Women Quarterly* 15:7–14.

La France, Marianne, and Mahzarin Banaji. 1992. "Toward a Reconsideration of the Gender-Emotion Relationship." In *Emotion and Social Behavior*, edited by Margaret S. Clark. Newbury Park, CA: Sage Publication.

Lamanna, Mary Ann, and Agnes Riedman. 1991. *Marriages and Families*. Belmont, CA: Wadsworth.

Langer, G. 1990. "More and More, Women Say Men Aren't Such Nice Guys." *Daily Reflector* (Greenville, NC), April 26.

Lazarus, Richard S. 1991. *Emotion and Adaptation*. New York: Oxford University Press.

Lerner, Harriet Goldhor. 1985. *The Dance of Anger*. New York: Harper and Row.

Levine, Judith. 1993. *My Enemy, My Love*. New York: Anchor Books.

Lewin, Tamar. 1994. "Teen Boys Still Expect to Be the Breadwinner." *News and Observer* (Raleigh, NC), July 24, 15A.

Lorber, Judith. 1994. *Paradoxes of Gender*. New Haven: Yale University Press.

Melani, Lilia, and Linda Fodaski. 1974. "The Psychology of the Rapist and His Victim." In *Rape: The First Sourcebook for Women*, edited by Noreen Connell and Cassandra Wilson. New York: New American Library.

Mirowsky, John, and Catherine E. Ross. 1995. "Sex Differences in Distress: Real or Artifact?" *American Sociological Review* 60:449–68.

Morin, Richard, and Megan Rosenfeld. 1998. "Men and Women, What Still Divides Us?" *News and Observer* (Raleigh, NC), April 19.

Novaco, Raymond W. 1976. "The Fuctions and Regulation of the Arousal of Anger." *American Journal of Psychiatry* 133:1124–28.

Philpot, Carol L., Gary R. Brooks, Don-David Lusterman, and Roberta L. Nutt. 1997. *Bridging Separate Gender Worlds*. Washington, D.C.: American Psychological Association.

Pollak, Lauren H., and Peggy A. Thoits. 1989. "Process in Emotional Socialization." *Social Psychology Quarterly* 52(1):22–34.

Reiser, Christa. 1993. "Gender Hostility: The Continuing Battle Between the Sexes." *Free Inquiry in Creative Sociology* 21:207–12.

———. 1994. "Sex, Gender Roles, and Perceptions of Anger." Unpublished.

———. 1995. "Gender Hostility: An Uneasy Truce." *College Student Journal* 29(2): 195–201.

Rook, Karen S. 1995. "Relationship Research at the Crossroads: Commentary on the Special Section." *Journal of Social and Personal Relationships* 12(4):601–6.

Rusting, Cheryl L., and Susan Nolen-Hoeksema. 1998. "Regulating Responses to Anger: Effects of Rumination and Distraction on Angry Mood." *Journal of Personality and Social Psychology* 74:790–803.

Sapiro, Virginia. 1990. *Women in American Society*. Mountain View, CA: Mayfield.

Shields, Stephanie A. 1987. "Women, Men, and the Dilemma of Emotion." In *Sex and Gender*, edited by P. Shaver and C. Hendrick. Beverly Hills, CA: Sage.

Shorter, Edward. 1975. *The Making of the Modern Family*. New York: Basic Books.

Shott, Susan. 1979. "Emotion and Social Life: A Symbolic Interactionist Analysis." *American Journal of Sociology* 84:1317–34.

Siegel, Judith M. 1986. "The Multidimensional Anger Inventory." *Journal of Personality and Social Psychology* 51(1):191–200.

Smith, Joan. 1992. *Misogynies*. New York: Ballantine Books.

Smith-Lovin, Lynn. 1989. "Sentiment, Affect, and Emotion." *Social Psychology Quarterly* 52(1):v–xii.

————. 1995. "The Sociology of Affect and Emotion." In *Sociological Perspectives on Social Psychology*, edited by Gary Alan Fine, Karen S. Cook, and James S. House. Needham Heights, MA: Allyn and Bacon.

Smucker, Carol, June Martin, and Dorothy Wilt. 1993. "Values and Anger." In *Women & Anger* (pp. 129–53), edited by Sandra P. Thomas. New York: Springer Publishing Company.

Spain, Daphne, and Suzanne M. Bianchi. 1996. *Balancing Act*. New York: Russell Sage Foundation.

Sprecher, Susan. 1986. "The Relation Between Inequity and Emotions in Close Relationships." *Social Psychology Quarterly* 49(4):309–21.

Stark-Adamec, Connie, and Robert E. Adamec. 1982. "Aggression by Men Against Women: Adaptation or Aberration?" *International Journal of Women's Studies* 5:1–21.

Stearns, Carol Z., and Peter N. Stearns. 1986. *Anger: The Struggle for Emotional Control in America's History*. Chicago: University of Chicago Press.

Stover, Ronald G., and Christine A. Hope. 1993. *Marriage, Family and Intimate Relations*. San Diego: Harcourt Brace Jovanovich.

Strong, Bryan, Christine DeVault, and Barbara W. Sayad. 1998. *The Marriage and Family Experience*. Belmont, CA: Wadsworth.

Tannen, Deborah. 1990. *You Just Don't Understand*. New York: Ballantine Books.

Tavris, Carole. 1989. *Anger, The Misunderstood Emotion*. New York: Simon & Schuster.

————. 1992. *The Mismeasure of Woman*. New York: Simon & Schuster.

Tedeschi, James T., and Richard B. Felson. 1994. *Violence, Aggression, and Coercive Actions*. Washington, D.C.: American Psychological Association.

Tedeschi, James T., and Mitchell S. Nesler. 1993. "Grievances: Development and Reactions." In *Aggression and Violence*, edited by Richard B. Felson and James T. Tedeschi. Washington D.C.: American Psychological Association.

Thoits, Peggy A. 1989. "The Sociology of Emotions." *Annual Review of Sociology* 15:317–42.

Thomas, Sandra P., ed. 1993. *Women & Anger*. New York: Springer Publishing Company.

Tomkins, Silvin S. 1991. *Affect, Imagery, and Consciousness: Vol. 30, The Negative Affects: Anger and Fear*. New York: Springer.

vos Savant, Marilyn. 1996. "Quotable Quotes." *Reader's Digest*, September, 161.

Walczak, Yvette. 1988. *He and She: Men in the Eighties*. New York: Routledge.

Walster, Elaine G., William Walster, and Ellen Berscheid. 1978. *Equity: Theory and Research*. Boston: Allyn and Bacon.

Washington Post. 1997. "Army to Charge Fitness Standards." September 15, A1, A7.

Wiggings, Beverly. 1993. Southern Focus Poll. Center for the Study of the American South Institute for Research in Social Science, University of North Carolina at Chapel Hill.

Williams, Redford, and Virginia Williams. 1993. *When Anger Kills*. New York: Harper Collins.

Wood, Julia T. 1994. *Gendered Lives: Communication, Gender and Culture*. Belmont, CA: Wadsworth.

Zillman, Dorf. 1979. *Hostility and Aggression*. New York: Erlbaum.

Index

About the Author

CHRISTA REISER is Associate Professor of Sociology at East Carolina University in Greenville, NC. She has a long-standing political and professional interest in gender issues. In addition to presenting papers, she has published several journal articles in this area.

ISBN 0-275-95777-2

90000>

EAN

9 780275 957773

HARDCOVER BAR CODE